PRAISE FOR *BEYOND PIGGY BANKS AND LEMONADE STANDS*

"Liz Frazier has written an engaging, must-read guide for parents on how to teach a critical life skill–healthy financial habits–with their children. Filled with relevant facts, family activities and suggested discussions, parents and children alike can learn smart money skills." —Shara Nadler, founder and CEO, iPiggiBank (ipiggibank.com), and mother of three

"In clear and simple terms, and within the context of everyday activities and fun games, Liz Frazier lays the foundation for children to develop financial literacy. Her thesis is clear: children, as young as preschoolers, should begin to be taught to recognize the value of money and how to avoid potential pitfalls as they mature. This book provides ideas, strategies and resources to guide parents as to how best prepare children to emerge as smart consumers and financially healthy adults."—Risa Tabacoff, PhD, MPS, MS, mother of three

"*Beyond Lemonade Stands and Piggy Banks: How to Teach Young Kids about Finance (and They're Never Too Young)* is a comprehensive yet easy to read guide. What better gift can we give our children than the ability to plan for and make smart choices about their future? As a teacher and parent, I appreciate the literary connections and online resources to support the lessons taught. I especially value the use of real life activities that parents can engage their child in at every developmental stage. This book inspires parents and teachers to teach children how to problem solve and learn finance for themselves through real hands-on experiences."—Victoria Lodewick, kindergarten teacher, and mother of three

"Liz Frazier's *Beyond Piggy Banks and Lemonade Stands* provides an easy-to-follow roadmap for parents to teach financial literacy to their elementary-aged kids. Comprehensive and detailed, it still allows the flexibility of depth and subjects, based on each child's skills and interest. Liz's humor coupled with interesting facts makes a seemingly daunting and complex subject an easy and light-hearted read, without the need for a background in financial knowledge. A great resource for all parents!" —Dina Shoman, founder and CEO, inherQuests

Beyond Piggy Banks and Lemonade Stands

Beyond Piggy Banks and Lemonade Stands

How to Teach Young Kids About Finance (and They're Never Too Young)

Liz Frazier

ROWMAN & LITTLEFIELD
Lanham • Boulder • New York • London

Published by Rowman & Littlefield
An imprint of The Rowman & Littlefield Publishing Group, Inc.
4501 Forbes Boulevard, Suite 200, Lanham, Maryland 20706
www.rowman.com

6 Tinworth Street, London SE11 5AL, United Kingdom

British Library Cataloguing in Publication Information Available

Library of Congress Cataloging-in-Publication Data

Names: Frazier, Liz, 1976– author.
Title: Beyond piggy banks and lemonade stands : how to teach young kids about
    finance (and they're never too young) / Liz Frazier.
Description: Lanham : Rowman & Littlefield, [2019] | Includes bibliographical
    references and index. |
Identifiers: LCCN 2019010815 (print) | LCCN 2019020348 (ebook) | ISBN
    9781475847635 (electronic) | ISBN 9781475847611 (cloth : alk. paper)
Subjects: LCSH: Financial literacy. | Finance, Personal—Study and teaching.
    | Children—Finance, Personal.
Classification: LCC HG179 (ebook) | LCC HG179 .F7227 2019 (print) | DDC
    332.0240083—dc23
LC record available at https://lccn.loc.gov/2019010815

Contents

**Part II: Getting Started with Money: Beginner Level:
Pre-K–First Grade**

**Part III: Piggy Bank Basics (Save, Share, and Spend):
Intermediate Level: 1st–5th Grade**

Foreword

When my son and daughter were preteens, my wife's job took her out of town for one evening each week, and it was my responsibility to provide dinner. Sometimes, the kids and I would go to the local K&W Cafeteria. My rule was that they got to choose their own meals—most anything reasonably healthy, but with the proviso that the total cost had to be under $2. (This was quite a while ago!)

They scanned the wide array of offerings and did the math, somehow always managing to pay for a yummy dessert along with the veggies and entrée. They enjoyed the challenge and learned something about how to manage a budget. With this experience in mind, I was entirely receptive to the main message of Liz Frazier's new book.

Specifically, the book is about how to teach your kids financial literacy. That may seem like a daunting task until you read what she has to say. With her guidance, the basic lessons are quite simple and can be taught through games and everyday challenges that they will enjoy. Of course, she goes a lot further than figuring out how to budget for key lime pie at K&W, but that's a start!

I've known Liz all her life and really can't imagine anyone better qualified to write this book—in a literal sense, she was born to it. She grew up in a close-knit family (and now she herself is a mother of two lively children). Her mom's a financial adviser, and her dad's a psychiatrist. Along her own way, Liz picked up an MBA, worked in business, and after a rigorous certification program, joined her mom and brother as a personal financial adviser. She also comes naturally by her sense of humor, as anyone who has enjoyed hanging out with her dad would agree.

If you have seen her articles on Forbes.com, you are already familiar with her good-humored common sense when it comes to finances and families.

Since I'm an economist, I need to say something about the context for this book. A majority of American families have little or nothing saved for retirement—or any other purpose, for that matter. This sad situation is *not* because they're ignoring the problem—in fact, financial concerns, from college age on, are a leading source of anxiety and all sorts of other troubles. What folks generally lack is the training and good habits that are most easily acquired when young.

Liz Frazier shows parents how they can help their kids avoid the anxiety and make a better life for themselves.

Philip J. Cook
Professor Emeritus of Public Policy and Economics
Duke University
October 2018

Preface

As parents, we understand the importance of talking to our young children about health and proper nutrition. We get them involved in sports to teach them the value of teamwork and exercise. We are told to start talking about the dangers of drugs with our children at a very early age. Yet with all this communication, somehow money is still considered taboo. Rarely are parents encouraged to sit down with their children to discuss the importance of budgeting or saving money.

When it comes to talking with our kids about finance, we don't want to stress them out or feel that they don't need to understand finance until they are older. And many people still think talking about money is just plain rude. Yet every step our kids take from college through retirement will be directly influenced by their ability to manage their finances: student loans, credit cards, jobs, mortgages, savings, and so on. Once they hit 18 years old, they are required, and able, to make decisions that could affect their entire life, often without the necessary knowledge and skills.

Being a financial planner to families, many who are struggling, I quickly saw the importance of having a basic financial education. So many of our adult issues could be avoided if we learned the importance of saving, avoiding debt, and how to spend responsibly at an early age. What started with some basic financial lessons for my own children quickly grew into a passion for getting children started on the right track.

I know what you're thinking. "Between school, homework, trying to have a social life, my job, their endless afterschool activities, my second job as an unpaid chauffer, incorporating more protein into my child's diet, family time . . . how in the world do you expect me to fit in regular finance lessons?"

I am fully with you. Like most of you, I'm a parent constantly pulled in a million directions trying to do what's best for my children (while trying to squeeze in a personal and professional life as well). My bottomless pit of to-do's actually includes something from two years ago (I really should just give up on "learn to make a quiche"). My plate is beyond full, so my goal is not to add to yours.

Beyond Piggy Banks and Lemonade Stands is meant to help parents change the way they think about finance and how they approach it with their children. The lessons provided are simple to teach and understand. The activities are quick, enjoyable, and educational. Each concept taught starts with the basics and builds upon them so your children have a full understanding. The chapters are broken out into simple and digestible sections, made for busy parents who don't have time for a finance novel. Each section specifies a basic appropriate age range for the topics—but of course, go at your children's pace. Some are ready earlier, and some need more time. Most of all, the book focuses on how to incorporate teaching finance to your children through *everyday real-world activities that you and your children are already doing.*

Every lesson, activity, and concept taught within this book is based around the following three goals:

1. Provide parents with the confidence to teach simple financial basics to children. With that confidence comes excitement and inspiration; by teaching your children about finance, you will influence every step of their lives in a positive and meaningful way.
2. Set a foundation for your children of basic financial understanding and smart decision-making that they can use and build upon for the rest of their lives.
3. The ultimate goal of this book, and of any parent, is to raise healthy, independent, and responsible children; kids who are prepared when adulthood hits!

For my overachiever parents (you know who you are!), keep in mind as you read this book: You are not going to "teach your children finance" in one sitting or in one week, one month, or even one year. Understanding finance is an ongoing, lifelong process. So don't put too much pressure on your children (or yourself) to conquer this book immediately. Take your time. After each chapter, allow your children to absorb what they learn and put it into practice before starting the next one.

Your next concern is an obvious and understandable one: "A book about finance? This will be painfully boring." Let's face it, most parents don't usually buy a book that teaches their children "financial literacy" as a fun summer read. I get it. This book embraces the craziness of children and encourages parents to laugh (even when they feel like crying). And really, what's funnier than being a parent and dealing with the daily absurdities that go along with it?

Enjoy and thanks for reading!

Acknowledgments

When I was in my 20s, I wanted to be an actress. After my first role as an extra in *Dawson's Creek*, I basically had my Oscar acceptance speech written out.

I may not have become the next Meryl Streep, but I finally get my Oscar speech . . .

First, I have to thank my mom, Deborah Frazier, who inspired me to become a financial planner and write this book. From a young age, you instilled the confidence in me that anything was possible and taught me through example the importance of independence, strength, and kindness. You are my role model as a mother, and every day my goal is to try to show my children half of the unconditional love and support you've given to me.

To my husband, Mike Peck: Thanks for reading, rereading, then rereading again my many book drafts, letting the children beat up on you so I can have "just five more minutes!," being a true partner, and always making me laugh. I'm sorry that you now know more than you ever wanted to know about finance.

To my sweet and wonderful kids: My favorite times in life are spent looking for dinosaurs with Owen, going on "movie dates" with Maddie, and being schooled in cooking by Mason. Or just cuddling with you guys on the couch will do any day. You are my heart, soul, and everything in-between. I love you to the moon and back. Thanks for being my guinea pigs for this book.

Thanks to all my friends and family from New York, North Carolina, and beyond who have listened to me obsess over this book for a year and provided me with many girls' trips, wine night escapes, and too many laughs to count. And lots of love. A special thanks to my Frazier clan: You are my true "Major Award."

Thank you to my publisher, Rowman & Littlefield, and especially to my editor, Sarah Jubar, who gave me the opportunity and confidence to write this book. Thank you to my designer, Kristen Buchholz, for her talented design work.

Thanks—I lucked out with you all.

Oh, and of course . . . I'd like to thank the Academy.

Part I

TIPS FOR THE ALREADY OVERWHELMED PARENT

1

Why Teach Finance to Elementary Aged Children?

It's the day that so many children (and parents) live for. Your children turn 18, and the world opens up to them! They can vote for president, enlist in the army, go skydiving, and be a part of jury duty! The world is their oyster and the possibilities are endless.

But wait, there's more. They can also sign a lease, be legally responsible for signing a contract, open a bank account, and get a credit card. For even the most responsible 18-year-old . . . well, this is a lot of responsibility. Specifically, these are responsibilities and decisions that come with real-life financial consequences that can have long-term effects.

At 18 years old, kids are thrust out into a world where every step they take from graduation to retirement will be directly affected by their financial knowledge and money management skills. Career decisions, buying the first house, getting married, having children—finances all play a massive role in each of these life events. Will your children be ready to make these kinds of decisions?

You are probably saying to yourself, "My child is only six; I have plenty of time to teach her." True, but you may be surprised to know that money habits can be formed as early as seven years old! Starting to introduce concepts and teach financial literacy to children at a young age is critical to their financial health as adults. Settle in and read why.

WHAT IS FINANCIAL LITERACY?

Financial literacy is a term most have heard but probably don't know exactly what it means. The President's Advisory Council on Financial

Literacy defines financial literacy as "the ability to use knowledge and skills to manage financial resources effectively for a lifetime of financial well-being" (*2008 Annual Report to the President,* https://www.treasury.gov/about/organizational-structure/offices/Domestic-Finance/Documents/exec_sum.pdf).

Financial literacy is just a fancy term to describe the ability to understand money and how it works. It includes a wide spectrum of money management: everything from the analysis of investment portfolios, to planning for retirement, to managing your daily grocery budget. Being financially literate includes the ability to plan for long-term goals like retirement and short-term goals like a weekend getaway.

If finance is not your strength and just reading these first few paragraphs gives you heart palpitations, you are in the majority. A 2015 study by the Financial Industry Regulatory Authority (FINRA) found that nearly two thirds of Americans couldn't pass a basic financial literacy test, meaning they got fewer than four answers correct on a five-question quiz. Worse, the percentage of those who can pass the test has fallen consistently since the financial crisis from 42% in 2009 to 37% in 2017.[1]

If you fall into this category, you have nothing to be ashamed of. It's not your fault because you probably weren't taught finance as a child and had to just figure it out as an adult. Not that it's really even your parents' fault for not teaching you the basics. Finances are intimidating and can be complex, and, until recently, there simply has not been a focus on financial education for young people. Thus, the issue. Thus, this book.

However, you can change all of this with the next generation.

WHY IS FINANCIAL LITERACY IMPORTANT FOR ADULTS?

The sole purpose in teaching children finance is so they can understand it and use this knowledge as an adult. But do adults *really* need to understand finance? As shown above, lots of people get by in their lives without understanding proper money management, right? Plus, many probably have a spouse who is the "finance-y" one, so they can take care of everything.

Well ... technically, yes, not knowing the proper way to create a budget probably will not *kill* you. However, understanding how to manage your finances can dramatically improve your life and prevent hardships in the future. And it's up to each and every adult to have this base knowledge so they have the confidence of knowing they can take care of themselves financially if needed.

Finances are understandably one of the major causes of stress for adults. Everyone can relate to this stress; even the wealthiest people have felt financial pains at one time or another. Debt and/or a lack of savings can cause considerable hardship on a person's life. And it doesn't just cause daily stress. Financial problems can lead to divorce, poor health, depression, and bankruptcy. The statistics below show that plenty of adults are feeling the pressure of financial issues. Many of these issues could be avoided with some basic knowledge.

- Nearly half of Americans don't have enough cash available to cover a $400 emergency.[2] Getting fired or having a medical emergency without any savings would be devastating. Understanding the importance of an emergency fund could prevent this.
- Millennials are starting their careers with a combined $1.1 trillion in debt.[3] Students coming out of college have more crippling student loans than ever. They are spending years trying to pay them off, which means they are saving less than they could. Being taught about debt, the different ways to pay for colleges, and the importance of not borrowing more than you can afford could help to prevent these massive numbers.
- Thirty-eight percent of US households have credit card debt. On average, they owe $16,048 with an APR of 16.47%.[4] While some debt, such as mortgages or student loans, can be considered "good" debt, credit cards are most definitely not. Learning the dangers of credit cards and high interest rates is critical as well as the importance of paying them off.
- Thirty-three percent of American adults have $0 saved for retirement.[5] Considering the fact that most will need at least $1 million to retire (for 30 years of living), a lack of savings is a major problem. The most important rule in saving for retirement is to start early. However, seldom do because they weren't taught the importance of compound interest and time.

These statistics are not meant to scare you but meant to show you how vital financial education is to living a financially healthy life. A study conducted by financial services company TIAA-CREF found a direct correlation between financial literacy and wealth.[6] It showed that those with high financial literacy plan for retirement and have double the wealth of people who do not plan for retirement. Those with low financial literacy borrow more, have less wealth, and end up paying unnecessary fees for financial products.

All of this can sound intimidating, but you don't have to be a sophisticated investor to understand enough about finance to be financially healthy. Being financially healthy means you know the difference between good debt and bad debt and know how to avoid crushing credit card debt. You understand the importance of saving often and early so as retirement nears you feel secure in your future. It also means that no matter your stage of life or income, you know how to live within your means, stick to a budget, and spend responsibly. Finally, healthy attitudes and confidence around money enable you to learn complex concepts, such as investing, and how to make smart decisions to make more money.

Just think if everyone learned finance as a child . . .

WHY TEACH KIDS *SO YOUNG*?

Anyone ever try to teach a 14-year-old who has never seen water to swim? Anyone ever just take their 14-year-old and throw him or her in the deep end of the pool, assuming that he or she will figure it out? Probably not, and for good reason. Swimming takes baby steps. Parents start basic water training early so their children are exposed to water and feel comfortable in it. As they get older, they have the confidence to learn and develop their swimming skills. And while most kids won't become the next Michael Phelps, that's not really the point. Swimming is a necessary skill to protect your children and make their lives more enjoyable.

OK, so no one has ever died from a lack of economics knowledge, but financial management should be seen as another important life skill (like knowing how to swim) that needs to be started early. As terrifying as this sounds, studies have shown that money habits have been formed as early as age seven! No pressure.

"The habits of mind, which influence the ways children approach complex problems and decisions, including financial ones, are largely determined in the first years of life," says David Whitebread, a psychologist and the co-author of the *Habit Formation and Learning in Young Children Study*.[7] This study shows that most children by the age of seven should know how to recognize the value of money and be able to count it out. They also can understand how money can be exchanged for products and what it means to earn money through work.

Most parents feel there is no way their seven-year-old is going to comprehend what a bank does or how interest is determined. Don't underestimate your children. Remember the last time you said a curse word in front of them or promised them they would get a bike next year? It's shocking (and often inconvenient) what children can learn and remember, especially when they don't seem to be paying attention.

A REAL-LIFE EXAMPLE (KIND OF)

Remember way back in the beginning of the chapter when the joys of adulthood were discussed? Refer to the example in Textbox 1.1 about Josh,

TEXTBOX 1.1. FINANCIAL PATHS

The Path of "Nonfinancial Josh"

This Josh wasn't exposed to finance and money when he was young. As he got older, he learned some of the basics, but finance was just something he didn't think about.

Upon graduation, Josh sets out to rent his first apartment. He's bringing home $2,500 net each month with his first job. He finds an apartment he loves, costing $1,500/month. He does some quick math, estimating his monthly bills, food, and car will be about $750, and decides he can afford it. Having never learned the importance of budgeting, he failed to consider entertainment, travel, work clothes he will need, household supplies, and so on.

The first few months are OK, but soon he realizes he's stretched too thin and isn't able to do a lot of what he enjoys. He decides to get a credit card, just to use for the occasional extras. After a year of putting "extras" on his card, he's racked up $2,735 in debt. In addition to having this debt weighing on him, he's also now got credit card payments to add to his expenses. All he can afford is the minimum, which is $68/month.

Since Josh is young and hasn't built up his credit yet, his interest rate is 19%. *If Josh continues paying only the minimums on his card, it will take him 228 months to pay off the card (that's 19 years!), and he will have paid a total of almost $7,000. Because he's paying off debt, he doesn't have any money left over for savings.*

The Path of "Financially Literate Josh"

Now, let's consider Josh's path if he had been taught about the financial basics growing up and understood the importance of saving and budgeting as well as the dangers of debt.

Upon graduation, Josh sets out to rent his first apartment. He's bringing home $2,500 net each month with his first job. He finds an apartment he loves, costing $1,500/month. He whips out his budget and runs the numbers. His monthly bills, food, and car will be about $750, leaving him with $250 each month. Then, he factors in his discretionary expenses, such as travel, entertainment, work clothes, and household supplies and realizes that realistically he will be stretched way too thin. In addition, he won't be able to save a cent. He has always put aside some of his money into savings, and it's important for him to continue doing so (his mom's so proud).

Josh chooses the runner-up apartment, which isn't his dream place but will do, and only costs $1,100/month. He's able to spend less total than what he earns and saves $68 each month. *In the same time frame as "Nonfinancial Josh" finally paid off his credit card (228 months), Josh has managed to save $28,504 (at a 6% interest rate).*

a young college graduate just entering the adult world. Depending on his financial knowledge experience and savvy, he could take one of two paths.

While this is clearly oversimplified, it has to be for purposes of comparing apples to apples. You may also be thinking to yourself "This is an extreme example." Sadly, it is not extreme at all. His credit card debt amount wasn't a random hypothetical; the average credit card debt for people between 25 and 34 years old is $2,735.[8] This is an all too true and common story for young people just getting started with their adult lives. The first Josh isn't necessarily desolate; he's still making ends meet . . . but he could be doing so much better! That $28,000 could be a down payment on a first house or go toward his retirement savings. All he needed was the right tools and knowledge.

TRENDS AFFECTING THE NEXT GENERATION

Back in my day, we used cash, there was no World Wide Web, and we walked uphill to school both ways. The times they are a changin'. As this generation matures, they will be faced with complexities and decisions that parents today never faced—providing even more incentives to learn money management.

- *The way consumers shop has changed.* Cash is being used less and less, and online shopping is now the preferred choice for many. More plastic and less cash lead to greater chances for this generation to use credit cards and accumulate debt.
- *Credit card companies are marketing geniuses.* OK, maybe not *geniuses*, but they sure are persistent. How is it every time you open the mail or click on a link, there's a credit card offer? Credit cards are making it easier than ever to get a credit card and rack up debt.
- *Social Security decrease.* Social Security was a safety net for generations past and still provides a major source of income for current retirees. However, it is underfunded, and many experts believe it's possible it will run out in the future. Others believe that, at the very least, the amount available will decrease dramatically. Regardless, kids today shouldn't depend on this as a substantial source of retirement income in the future.
- *Complex options and decisions.* Many of those in generations past had the luxury of a pension; they didn't have to manage their retirement investments and knew exactly how much they would receive in retirement. Today, many don't even know what a pension is, let alone have one. Most people have retirement plans, such as 401(k)s, which require being actively involved in managing their investments. With hundreds of options, including stocks, mutual funds, index funds,

and target date funds, it's easy to become overwhelmed with the decisions and not always make the best choices.

SOME SILVER LININGS

Enough of the scare tactics. Let's focus on all the positives that come *with* financial education.

- *Promote good saving habits.* Josh's story in this chapter provided an example of the good that can come out of saving early. Just imagine if your children came out of college and started immediately saving for their future.
- *Budgeting teaches awareness and responsibility.* If people have budgets that they actively manage, it forces them to look at their spending. They are aware of how much they have available, and this leads to making better spending decisions.
- *Smart financial decisions positively affect one's credit score.* Kids and even young adults don't understand the concept of credit scores They don't realize that their credit will affect their daily lives: getting a job, applying for a credit card, renting an apartment, buying a home or car, getting insurance, or even signing up for their power bill. Having an excellent credit score could save them thousands and thousands of dollars in interest payments over their lifetime.
- *What's good for them is good for the parents.* Isn't this the truth in every way? As of 2016, 15% of 25- to 35-year-olds were living in their parents' home.[9] This is an increase from the previous generation. Moving back home for a short break is not always a bad thing; it can allow young adults to recalibrate and get organized. However, often, the reason the "children" move back home with their parents is for financial support. So the more educated your children are about finance, the less likely they are to need money, and the less money you, as a parent, will need to spend. Win, win, and win.
- *More jobs, more money, and less debt are good for the economy as a whole.* This will be covered in Chapter 11. Oh yes, your children will learn economics.
- *Teaches giving back.* Incorporating the importance of charity at a young age coupled with better financial management skills provides people with more money and a desire to give back. This benefits not only the community but the children as well; charitable giving promotes confidence and compassion.
- *Less debt.* If your children understand how to budget, they will be more likely to live within their means and not go into debt. This means they avoid the suffocating stress that comes with it.

- *Positive communication skills.* Because you communicated with your children about finance, they will learn lessons in positive communication around finance. This will be incredibly valuable as they get older, especially with their spouses.
- *Financially healthy attitude.* If your children are taught positive money management and how to be financially healthy, they are more likely to develop positive attitudes around money and wealth. People's attitudes around money can be instrumental in shaping their characters. Below are examples of financially healthy attitudes.

  ○ I understand that having money isn't good or bad. Money is neutral. It is a tool to help me reach my goals.
  ○ Giving back is important to me, and I make it a priority.
  ○ I am grateful for what I have.
  ○ I'm not envious of others and don't compare myself financially to them. I know that most people project their best side. Gary and Lisa from next door may have a gorgeous house and expensive cars, but they could be up to their noses in debt paying for them. You just never know . . . and it doesn't matter to me anyway.
  ○ I not only value hard work, I value *smart* work.

WON'T THEY LEARN FINANCE IN SCHOOL?

As of today . . . probably not. They should, but sadly most don't. According to a report by the Consumer Financial Protection Bureau (CFPB), childhood financial attitudes, habits, and norms develop between the ages of 6 and 12, yet it's not a part of elementary schools' standard curriculum. It's no surprise that a financial literacy test given by the National Financial Educators Council found that test takers from 15–18 years old scored an average of only 61%.[10]

It seems ludicrous right? High schools teach geometry, art, foreign language, and European history—all valuable subjects to know, for sure. But how is it possible that most don't offer personal finance as a class? We already know that every step students take after graduation will be affected by their ability to manage money. How often on a day-to-day basis do you need to calculate the area of a trapezoid (FYI—because now you're curious: the area of a trapezoid = $(a + b) / 2 \times h$).

The point being, finance is not a mandatory high school course in most states. In fact, only 17 states require that high school students take a finance course (and "finance" could be a loose term). And forget about elementary or middle school; it's not even on the *radar* of most schools.

The good news is that since 2013, the CFPB, among other individuals and organizations, has been pushing for regulations requiring all 50 states to mandate financial literacy training for kids in elementary and secondary schools. The CFPB created *Transforming the Financial Lives of a Generation of Young Americans*, which includes the following specific recommendations for advancing financial education in grades K–12.[11]

1. Teach financial education early and consistently through K–12 years
2. Introduce financial education concepts into standardized tests
3. Create innovative hands-on learning opportunities
4. Create consistent opportunities and incentives for teacher training
5. Encourage parents to discuss money management topics at home

The 2017 Financial Report Card from Champlain College's Center for Financial Literacy provides the grades for all states, based on their efforts to produce financially literate high school graduates. Sadly, only five states received an "A" grade for their financial education efforts: Alabama, Missouri, Tennessee, Utah, and Virginia. These five states require high school students to take at least a half-year personal finance course as a graduation requirement.

The report card gave a "B" to 19 states that require students to receive personal finance instruction to graduate from high school, but the standards are a bit more flexible than those of the "A" states. The map shown in Figure 1.1 shows how the remaining grades were distributed.

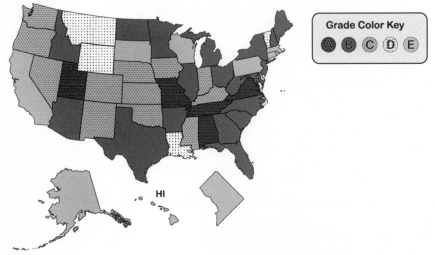

Figure 1.1. State Report Card. Champlain College's Center for Financial Literacy. *Kristen Buchholz.*

The study compared the states that had mandatory finance courses versus those that did not and found that the courses had a tangible effect on the students. "We find that if a rigorous financial education program is carefully implemented," the report stated, "it can improve the credit scores and lower the probability of delinquency for young adults."[12]

So this topic is clearly generating a lot of interest. There is more of a focus now among local and state policy makers, major federal agencies, and the media to push for teaching kids personal finance in schools. But we're not there yet. Until then, parents are the primary source of information for their kids. And the truth is, even *when* all schools teach personal finance to students, parents will continue to be the most influential source of information for their kids. Basically, you should still read this book.

SHORT AND SWEET TAKEAWAYS

1. As an adult, a basic understanding of finance will make your life easier in countless ways. It will help you stay out of debt, save for retirement, and live a more comfortable life . . . just to name a few.
2. Teaching kids early about financial literacy means they will have the foundation to continue learning about finance their whole lives. They won't be intimidated by finance and will be more likely to have positive and healthy attitudes around money. Then, when they become an adult . . . refer back to #1.
3. Children will probably not be taught financial literacy in school. Children *may* learn a wee bit of finance in high school but not enough. So it's up to the parents and caregivers to teach finance to their children.

NOTES

1. FINRA. 2015. "National Financial Capability Study: US Survey Data at a Glance." Accessed September 3, 2018. http://www.usfinancialcapability.org/results.php?region=US.

2. Federal Reserve. 2017. "Federal Reserve Board Issues Report on the Economic Well-Being of US Households." Accessed September 4, 2018. https://www.federalreserve.gov/newsevents/pressreleases/other20170519a.htm.

3. Hernandez, Raul. 2017. "Millennials owe a record amount of debt, and it could become a huge drag on the economy." *Business Insider*, April 29, 2017. http://www.businessinsider.com/record-millennial-debt-a-drag-on-the-economy-2017-4.

4. Frankel, Mathew. 2017. "Here's the average American's credit card debt—and how to get yours under control." *USA Today*, January 24, 2017. https://www

.usatoday.com/story/money/personalfinance/2017/01/24/heres-the-average-americans-credit-card-debt-and-how-to-get-yours-under-control/96611546/.

5. Kirkham, Elyssa. 2016. "1 in 3 Americans Has Saved $0 for Retirement." *Money*, March 14, 2016. http://time.com/money/4258451/retirement-savings-survey/.

6. TIAA-CREF Institute. 2011. "Wealth, Financial Literacy and Schooling." Accessed on September 3, 2018. https://www.tiaainstitute.org/sites/default/files/presentations/2017-02/ti_wealth0211a.pdf.

7. Whitebread, Dr. David, and Dr. Sue Ningham. 2013. *Habit Formation and Learning in Young Children.* Accessed September 3, 2018. https://mascdn.azureedge.net/cms/the-money-advice-service-habit-formation-and-learning-in-young-children-may2013.pdf.

8. Spinelle, Jenna. 2016. "A Breakdown of Millennial Debt & What the Numbers Look Like Now." Credit Sesame, July 26, 2016. https://www.creditsesame.com/blog/debt/breakdown-millennial-debt/.

9. Fry, Richard. 2017. "It's becoming more common for young adults to live at home – and for longer stretches." Pew Research Center, May 5, 2017. http://www.pewresearch.org/fact-tank/2017/05/05/its-becoming-more-common-for-young-adults-to-live-at-home-and-for-longer-stretches/.

10. National Financial Educators Council. 2018. "Financial Literacy Test & Survey Center." Accessed on September 4, 2018. https://www.financialeducatorscouncil.org/financial-literacy-test/.

11. CFPB. 2013. "Transforming the Financial Lives of a Generation of Young Americans." Accessed September 3, 2018. https://files.consumerfinance.gov/f/201304_cfpb_OFE-Policy-White-Paper-Final.pdf.

12. Champlain College. 2017. "Is Your State Making the Grade?" Accessed September 3, 2018. https://www.champlain.edu/centers-of-experience/center-for-financial-literacy/report-national-high-school-financial-literacy.

2

How to Make Teaching Finance to Kids Painless

As noted earlier, and reinforced throughout these chapters, the goal of this book is not to turn your children into financial geniuses by the time they graduate elementary school (mainly, because it's just not realistic). The financial universe is infinite and so complex that even professionals can't understand all of it. Your children will continue to learn about finance into adulthood. This is a journey, not a destination. The goal is to introduce them now to concepts and build the foundations for later learning.

For example, taxes will be touched on at this age. Children will understand by the end of the book that, when they make money, part of their money goes to the government. They will also understand what these taxes pay for. However, there will be no mentions of things like Alternate Minimum Tax or Mortgage Deductibles. The same depth of teaching goes for concepts like insurance, inflation, and credit cards. Because really, why would you want to teach your sweet eight-year-olds the details of topics that most adults don't even grasp? Let them keep their innocence for a little longer.

This book focuses on teaching age-appropriate financial basics: counting, earning, saving, spending, and sharing money. This chapter outlines the methods used to teach finance that will be used throughout the book as well as tips to keep in mind with each lesson.

TEACH/EXPLORE/DISCUSS

Throughout the book, each of the major concepts will be broken down through a simple three-step process: teach, explore, discuss.

1. *Teach.* Each section begins with simple ways for parents to explain the overall concept and basic terms to their children.
2. *Explore.* Once the parents have described the financial concept, the book provides the following hands-on ways for them to explore the material with their children. Because every child is different, multiple types of activities, games, and other creative ways are included. Only you know your children, so if one tactic doesn't work, try a different one.

   - *Everyday activities.* Think of this as sneaking in financial education. One of the best ways to teach children about money is to incorporate lessons and activities into everyday activities. Many of these activities take place at some sort of store because that's where you are using money. Since most parents would do anything to avoid taking their children to a store, don't try these store activities when you're in a hurry or at the end of the day, when your patience is running low.
   - *Games.* Because finance doesn't top the list of "fun weekend activities" for your nine-year-olds, it has to be entertaining. New and existing games are used throughout the book, all promoting interaction and making learning the information fun.
   - *Real-world activities.* The everyday activities and games are used solely for teaching purposes. The real-world activities put the lessons to work, will actually have a tangible effect on your children, and are things that people do in the real world. A perfect example of this is when your children open their first bank accounts, addressed in Chapter 9 about saving.
   - *Pretend play.* Kids love to pretend, and this type of play allows kids to participate firsthand in financial transactions. Games where kids can pretend are incorporated throughout the book by playing games such as store, restaurant, and work.
   - *Books.* Each chapter will have several children's book recommendations to provide further learning in a way that your children enjoy. The most valuable part of reading financially focused books is the discussion afterward. Ask your children open-ended questions, such as "What would you have done in that situation?" or "What could he have done differently?," or more specific questions, such as "Why do you think his mom was mad at him?"
   - *Scripts.* Every parent has been there. You stumble when your children stump you with a question. Or worse, they completely smooth talk their way out of a situation. There are clear areas throughout these financial lessons when communication problems can arise (such as how to respond to your children when they insist on buying that cheap Minion knock-off at the town fair).

Scripts or talking points will be provided for these tough spots to keep the conversation on track. That being said, all parents know children are masters at conversation diversion . . . so it's still necessary to be prepared for battle with some of these discussions! Also included are simple ways to explain complex terms and concepts.

3. *Discuss.* Finally, after each activity, parents are provided with quizzes and discussion points to encourage conversation and openness with their children. Ask them what interested them, what they didn't understand, and how it's relevant to their lives.

NEED TO LEARN MORE ABOUT FINANCE BEFORE YOU TEACH IT? THREE EASY STEPS TO PREPARE

If finance is not your thing and you're worried you don't know enough to teach your children, there are easy things you can do to prepare. To help you get organized and feel more confident in your own financial capabilities, go through the following exercises. Don't worry if it's not perfect; taking some time to think about the items will demystify "finance" and make it seem less intimidating. Just remember, you only have to understand some basics to live a financial healthy life.

1. *Know your finances.*
   Create a net worth statement, which is a snapshot of your financial world. How much do you have, and how much do you owe? A simple spreadsheet, like the one in Figure 2.1, can get you started.
   Next, create a budget. No one likes the "B" word, but it's not meant to be a form of torture. Figure 2.2 provides a simple budget example. It's just a record of how much you make and how much you spend. The two most important things to consider are pay yourself first and make sure you make more than you spend.
2. *Determine your goals.*
   Are you saving for a new house? Want to retire in five years? Or are you hoping to start your own business at some point? Get clear about your goals, determine if they are long term or short term, and prioritize them.
3. *Build positive habits.*
   Below are easy things you can do now to help manage your finances.

   - Automate your monthly savings
     - Contribute something to your company's 401(k) each month. Especially if they have a match program. You can start small; every little bit helps, and it gets you in the habit of saving.

NET WORTH STATEMENT

Assets

Cash		
	Checking	$1,000
	Savings	$3,000
	Other cash	
	Total Cash	*$4,000*
Investments		
	Stocks, bonds, mutual funds	$10,000
	Other investments	
	Total Investments	*$10,000*
Property		
	Real Estate	$200,000
	Auto	$5,000
	Jewelry, Art, Collectibles	
	Other property	
	Total Property	*$205,000*
Retirement		
	Retirement Accounts	$25,000
	Other retirement	
	Total Retirement	*$25,000*
	Total Assets	**$244,000**

Liabilities

	Mortgage	$120,000
	Auto Loans	$2,000
	Student Loans	$10,000
	Personal Loans	
	Other liabilities	
	Credit Card Debt	$2,000
	Total Liabilities	**$134,000**

Total Net Worth (Assets – Liabilities)	**$110,000**

Figure 2.1. Example of a Net Worth Statement. *Liz Frazier.*

Monthly Budget		
Income		
	Salary 1	$4,000
	Salary 2 (spouse)	$2,000
	Other income	
	Total Income	**$6,000**
Fixed Expenses		
	Mortgage	$2,500
	Power	$100
	Auto	$120
	Insurance	$100
	Cable	$80
	Water	$40
	Phone/Internet	$90
	Total Fixed Expenses	*$3,030*
Discretionary Expenses		
	Food	$800
	Clothing	$150
	Children Supplies	$100
	Gas	$40
	Child Care	$200
	Medical	$100
	Entertainment	$150
	Eating Out	$60
	Household Supplies	$120
	Travel	$150
	Repairs	$200
	Misc	$250
	Total Discretionary Expenses	*$2,320*
	Total Expenses	**$5,350**
	(Fixed + Discretionary)	
Savings		$600
Surplus / Deficit		
(Income – Total Expenses – Savings)		**$50**

Figure 2.2.   Example of a Monthly Budget Statement. *Liz Frazier.*

- ○ Start putting a little away each month for your children's education in your state's 529 program.
- Automate your bills
  - ○ Set aside an hour and set up auto draft on every bill so you are never late. This is especially important for credit cards.
- Pay extra on credit cards
  - ○ Make it a habit to pay a little more than the minimum payment each month, even if it's just an extra $20. By just making minimum payments, you are barely touching your principal, and it can take a long time to finally pay off the full balance.

THE IMPORTANCE OF TALKING WITH YOUR CHILDREN

Whether you intend it or not, your children are learning money habits and attitudes from you every day, both the good and the bad. Follow the guidelines below to be sure you are sending the right message.

1. *Set a positive example.* Like everything else in life, you are the most influential person in your child's world (again, no pressure). If you have a positive and healthy attitude about money, your children will learn the same. As you talk about money with or around your children, try to keep the following in mind: *Money isn't the root of all evil nor will it buy happiness. Money is a tool to help you reach your goals. It's not everything, but it is an important part of our life.*

   And it's not all about just being a positive role model. Just as important is avoiding being a negative example. Parents who have bad money habits are likely to pass them onto their children. Luckily, by committing to teaching your children finance, you are already working to positively influence them, and you may learn better financial habits yourself.

2. *Make money part of the conversation.* Make it a point to talk about money around your children. This doesn't mean complaining about money, and you don't need to talk about specifics, like your salary. Encourage openness by including finances in your normal daily conversations. Include them in your financial decisions and discuss some of your bills and purchases. Share your experiences, mistakes, and successes. It's OK to tell your children "I spent too much money on a credit card when I was 20 years old, and it took me a long time to pay it off" or "I started saving right out of college and was able to buy a house with the money I saved." Share the little things too: "I am so proud of myself; I sold my old books on eBay and made money!" Ask lots of questions, keep it nonjudgmental, and encourage discussion. Again, be sure to keep money talk neutral or positive; the last thing you want

is your children to worry about money. They won't understand everything you say, but they will pick up on any stress.

Ideally, these conversations will be part of the daily flow, but parents have a million things on their mind, and it's easy to forget. An easy and natural time to discuss money with your children is each week when you give them allowance (much more on allowance later). You can count their money together, see if their savings goals have changed, or talk about one of the financial decisions you had to make this week.

A STEP-BY-STEP GUIDE TO AGE-APPROPRIATE INFORMATION

While every child is different, Table 2.1 gives a basic idea of what financial concepts children can learn and understand by grade level. The book is structured to start with topics best suited for younger kids and

Table 2.1.   Appropriate Concepts by Grade Level

Grade	Appropriate Concepts
Kindergarten–2nd Grade	Understand what money is and how it's used
	Counting and comparing money
	Need money to buy things
	Understand value
	How to wait
	Identify coins
	Wants versus needs
	Reaching goals
	Compassion and giving
	Work to earn money
3rd–5th Grade	Deeper understanding of the different ways to make money
	Budgets
	Planning in advance
	Product pricing
	Charity and specific ways to give back
	Responsible spending
	Interest
	Saving and investing
	How to make decisions
	Advertising
	Debt and credit cards

Sources:
Morin, Amanda. n.d. "Typical Developmental Milestones for Grade-Schoolers: Developmental Milestones." Accessed September 1, 2018. https://www.understood.org/en/learning-attention-issues/signs-symptoms/developmental-milestones/developmental-milestones-for-grade-schoolers.
The President's Advisory Council on Financial Capability. n.d. "Money as You Grow." Accessed September 1, 2018. https://www.treasury.gov/resource-center/financial-education/Documents/Money%20as%20You%20Grow.pdf.
Scholastic. n.d. "Financial Literacy Lessons for Grades K-8." Accessed September 1, 2018. http://www.scholastic.com/browse/article.jsp?id=3757932.

get more challenging as they continue. Although each "part" of the book includes a recommended age range, go at your children's own pace and pay attention to their level of comprehension. The beginning may be more appropriate for grades kindergarten through first grade; however, you may have an older child just starting to learn about money. Or you may feel the older child needs a refresher. If that's the case, start at the beginning; a reminder never hurt anyone. Or the opposite may be true; your children may be in kindergarten but already understand the basic financial concepts that are taught early in the book. Go ahead and skip anything that your children may find boring and would demotivate them from wanting to learn more.

Parent tip. If you're teaching something to younger and older elementary school children at the same time, have the older one help "teach" the younger one. That way he or she doesn't feel like you are putting him or her in the same category with his or her little sibling (perish the thought!), and he or she is still learning.

INTERNET, APPS, AND DEBIT CARDS . . . OH MY!

We are getting closer and closer each year to becoming a completely cashless society. Most adults rely on debit and credit cards, digital wallets, online banking, and savings apps. Rarely do you pay for your groceries, dinner, or bills with cash. It's likely that electronic payment methods will become more widespread and the use of cash will continue to decline.

Electronic payments will be addressed with each chapter but not used for teaching purposes. It's easier for children to understand money if you start out teaching them with cash. Kids can hold coins and dollar bills, count them out, and engage in transactions directly with them. Digital money to a young child is too hypothetical. Most don't have direct access to online accounts, so they wouldn't use these tools until they are older anyway. Plus, technology is advancing exponentially, so the hot digital wallet today may be obsolete tomorrow. Once the basics are learned, digital tools will be addressed but not focused on.

SHORT AND SWEET TAKEAWAYS

1. Everyone is different. Some kids learn best by doing, some by seeing, and some by listening. If your child isn't getting something or isn't enjoying an activity, try a different one.

2. Don't let not understanding finance deter you from teaching your children. This book is made to be simple enough that young children can grasp the concepts. You will too.
3. And if you *still* don't feel comfortable with finances, there are some quick actions you can take to get your financial knowledge in order, like create a budget and determine your net worth.
4. Communicate! Gone are the days where it's considered "rude" to talk about money. Have open and positive communication with your children so financial management is a normal part of their everyday lives.
5. Go at your own pace, based on your children's age, knowledge, and experience.

Part II

GETTING STARTED WITH MONEY

Beginner Level: Pre-K–1st Grade

3

What Is Money?

Even the youngest kindergarteners probably have an idea of what money is. They see their parents use it to buy groceries, they hear them talk about it, and they may even get an allowance. However, the younger children may not know the difference between a nickel and a quarter yet or know all of the different ways that you can count change. Older elementary school children may understand the basics but still believe in the almighty money tree.

Never fear—this chapter covers it all! All you need are lots of coins, a few dollar bills, and basic math skills (or a calculator). There are several illustrations within this chapter to help if you don't have enough money on hand for some of the activities, but kids will learn best in the beginning by interacting with real coins.

By the end of this chapter, your children should understand the basics of money and how to count all different types. Included in this chapter are some simple math lessons teaching the different ways that money can be counted. The chapter ends with how money is actually made so your children stop assuming it grows on trees.

EXPLAINING MONEY

Kids understand as early as age three that money can be exchanged for something they want.[1] Start the conversation with your children by explaining that there wasn't always money. Before money, people used to exchange things other than money, which is called *bartering*. For example, if someone wanted a pig from her neighbor, she would give him five chickens. Or if she wanted to buy a loaf of bread, she would have to "pay" him with six eggs.

Tell your children it's similar to when they trade toys with their friends. Ask them if a friend wanted to borrow one of their LEGO sets, what would they want to trade it for? Point out that it would probably be something of similar value. Even though they didn't know it, they are "bartering" when they trade toys with friends. People started using coins and money because it was easier than trading things like cows, chickens, shells, and eggs. So now, if people want to buy a cow, they use money instead of chickens.

PLAY ARCHEOLOGIST WITH COINS

Before your children learn anything more about money, they have to learn their coins. This will probably be more relevant for the younger elementary school children, as the older ones have had more experience with coins. Your young children may or may not be able to identify each of the four major coins. This is the time for you to get out all your pocket change and coins between the cushions and from the car glove compartment. Make sure you have the big four represented (pennies, nickels, dimes, and quarters).

Start by dumping all your coins out on the table. Pretend like you are an archeologist. This should be no problem for your children because they approach the world naturally as budding scientists. Let them observe the coins without an agenda. Encourage them to touch the coins, stack them, spin them—let them use all their senses (except tasting, especially the coins from the couch cushions). If they can't identify each coin yet, just make sure you keep using the proper coin names over and over. "You're right, this nickel is very shiny" or "Yep, that penny is bigger than the dime."

Once your children have done some observing on their own, ask them to sort the coins. Most will naturally separate them by coin type: pennies, nickels, dimes, and quarters. Again, begin by observing these coins with your children, and start noting the differences between the coins. Ask your children questions about the different coins to help them get familiar with them. Below are some examples. Make sure they answer by using the coins' names, not just pointing to them:

- Which coins are silver?
- Can you find the numbers on each coin?
- What do the men look like on each coin? Which ones have long hair?

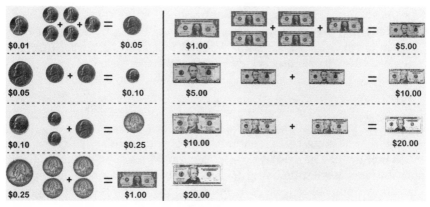

Figure 3.1. Guide to Money. *Kristen Buchholz.*

- Can you find a bird on one of the coins?
- Can you line the coins up from biggest to smallest?

If you want to review money with your children on the go, Figure 3.1 provides a visual guide to the different types of coins and bills.

Practice Activity: Drawing Coins

Have your children trace each of the four types of coins, two times per coin. Use only one piece of paper so they can see the difference in sizes. Then, have the children draw both the head and tail sides of each coin. Help them fill in details, like numbers and symbols, to help them later better identify coins.

Real-World Activity: Coin Collecting

Like any hobby, coin collecting can be a rewarding, fun, and educational activity for your children at any age; it's also an opportunity to spend time together. There is no wrong way to start a collection, and the ways to collect coins are endless. You and your children can start an inexpensive collection by collecting coins that are already in circulation or up the stakes and buy rare coins at coin shows and shops.

To start simply, begin by collecting a quarter from each state or a coin from each year. If you start a collection on your own, buy a coin folder to help sort and store your coins. These can be purchased (online or at a coin shop) for as low as $5.

For those parents who want to take it a step further, you can buy a book or set that will help guide you and your children into the coin collecting world, such as the ones below:

- *Coin Collecting for Kids Board Book* by Steve Otfinoski and Jack Graham
- Warman's has published several coin collecting books and starter sets, such as *State Quarters for Kids: 1999-2009* and *Jefferson Nickels for Kids: 1978-2012 Collector's Jefferson Nickel Folder*
- *State Series Quarter Map*, created by HE Harris

Discussion

As you're collecting coins, continue to ask your children to count how much money they have total in the collection. Make sure it's fun for them, and always ask what type of coin they want to collect next. Coin collecting can be a fun scavenger hunt, either around the house, at the store, or when you travel.

COUNTING COINS

If your children can count, they can count money. If they have trouble with counting, what better way for them to learn than with coins? Get all your coins back out and start off simply. Line up all the coins by value and remind your children what each one is worth. To illustrate this, next to the penny, put one penny. Next to the nickel, put five pennies, and so on. This may require a trip to a change machine by the time you get to a quarter!

Next, do the same with a nickel. Next to the nickel will be one nickel, next to the dime will be two nickels, and next to the quarter will be five nickels. Repeat the exercise with dimes. It's best to do this activity with actual coins because it's more engaging, but since some parents may not have 42 pennies lying around, refer back to Figure 3.1 to provide an abbreviated illustrated version.

Practice Activity: Counting Coins

Below are simple activities to do with your children to learn to count coins. Children learn at their own pace, so don't worry if they have trouble with these activities. The purpose of this activity is to introduce them to the basics and reinforce what they are learning; they will continue to learn as they go. The more they practice and play with coins, the easier it will be for them.

- Play a game, similar to the card game War. Mix up a bunch of coins in a bag. Both you and your children close your eyes and pick up a handful from the bag. Count how much you have, and whoever has the most money wins that round. Keep score of how much you each have with each round, and whoever reaches $5 first wins. Marshmallows or M&Ms always work well as a reward.

- Ask your children how they can make $.52 with the coins they have. Then, have them do it again with the same number, using different types of coins. Repeat this activity with several different amounts. You can also ask them different variations, such as "using only four coins, how can you make $.52?"
- This is a golden opportunity to help your children learn to count by 5s and 10s. Line up multiple dimes and help your children count by 10s; then, do the same with nickels.
- Create two piles of coins and ask your children which one is bigger by counting the number of coins. Then, with the same two piles, ask your children to figure out which one is *worth more* by counting the value. Examples are 10 pennies versus 3 dimes or 2 quarters versus 6 nickels.
- When you get change at the store or drive-through, ask your children to count it for you.
- Make up counting games as you go along, such as making treats "cost" money. If your children want cookies after dinner, tell them that will cost them $.31 (meaning they just have to figure out what coins they could use to come up with $.31, not that they actually have to pay).

Pop Quiz: Put Your Coin Counting to the Test

Respond to the following questions. (The answers are at the end of the book on page 145.)

1. What are three ways to make $.63?
2. How can you make $.37 using four coins? What about using 7 coins? Try one more time using 11 coins.
3. What's worth more: 1 quarter, 3 dimes, and 5 pennies OR 17 pennies and 1 dime?
4. How many nickels are in 2 quarters?

MOVING ON TO DOLLARS

Don't worry, for the next activity you don't need to withdraw $1,000 from the bank in equal denominations of ones, fives, tens, and twenties. Your children now have a base understanding of counting coins, so dollars should be a piece of cake. Have one example of each of the following bills:

one, five, ten, and twenty. Similar to the coin activities, start by simply ob-serving each dollar; identify the numbers, images, and symbols on each.

Repeat the coin counting activity, this time using a mix of dollars and coins. For example, next to the dollar, put four quarters. Next to the $5 bill, put five $1 bills, and so on. The different combinations of dollars and coins are endless; let your children play with them to create their own combinations.

Pop Quiz: Hidden Objects

After your children have looked at the different images and numbers on the bills, tell them that there are multiple "hidden" symbols and pictures on each bill. Have them find the answers to the questions below. (The answers are at the end of the book on page 145.)

1. Where is the eyeball?
2. Where is the eagle on each bill?
3. Which bill *doesn't* have an eagle on the front?
4. How many times can you find the number 13 on the dollar bill?
5. Which bill has the White House on the back?
6. Can you find the man sitting in a chair?
7. Can you find the hidden keys?
8. Which bill has a torch on the front?

Kids' Activity: Board Games

Board games are a fantastic way for kids to get their hands on money and to show them how to use money. As an extra bonus, they are a blast to play as a family.

- *Monopoly.* Who doesn't love this game? Although Monopoly can teach some fairly sophisticated economic concepts (to be discussed in later chapters), kids can also refine their basic skills in counting and under-standing the value of money. Plus, parents get to relive the glory days of snatching up Park Place and Boardwalk. If you don't have the board game, play it online for free on sites like www.poki.com.
- *Money Bags.* This game is perfect for teaching the concepts in this chapter. Kids practice valuable skills by counting coins, practicing addition and subtraction with money, and identifying coins.
- *Game of Life.* Do you have what it takes to win the Game of Life? Again, sophisticated concepts are taught in this game, but kids get hands-on money experience and have to make real-life money decisions.

WHERE DOES MONEY COME FROM?

The final piece of the money puzzle is to put it in context by showing your children that money is actually made—it doesn't just magically appear. There are several ways parents could go about doing this. You could take your young children to one of the US Mint or Bureau of Engraving and Printing facilities and get a tour. However, if the choice for your family summer vacation is between that or a beach trip, this could be a tough sell. It may be easier to explain how money is made.

There are two bureaus within the US Department of the Treasury responsible for making the coins and bills: The US Mint produces coins, and the Bureau of Engraving and Printing (BEP) produces paper currency.

HOW COINS ARE MADE

Coins are money made from metals. They used to be made from valuable metals, such as gold and silver. Today, most coins are made with some combination of copper, zinc, and nickel. US coins are made by the US Mint, which is a division of the Department of the Treasury. There are four US Mint facilities that make coins, located in Philadelphia, Denver, San Francisco, and New York.

In a very simplified nutshell, this is how a coin is created:

- *Step 1—Design.* New coins are designed by artists that work for the US Mint. They are called sculptor engravers.
- *Step 2—Create the models.* Sculptors then create a model of the coin. A plaster cast is made of the coin, which is then scanned into a computer. The computer software uses tools to create the coin dies, which are used later to stamp the design onto each coin.
- *Step 3—Manufacturing.*
  - *Blanking.* Long strips of metal are run through a blanking press, which cuts out blank coins from the press. Think of it like a giant cookie cutter.
  - *Annealing.* The blank coins then go through the annealing process, which heats up the coins and softens them.
  - *Upsetting.* The upsetting mill forms the raised rim you see around the edges of the coin.
  - *Striking.* The coining press strikes (or stamps) the design of the coin into the metal on both sides. They are then considered official US coins.

- ◦ *Inspecting.* Trained inspectors use magnifying glasses to examine the coins to make sure they were made correctly. Then, all the coins go through a coin sizer to remove any misshapen or dented ones.
- ◦ *Counting and bagging.* An automatic counting machine counts the coins and drops them into large canvas bags. The bags are shipped by truck to Federal Reserve Banks. From there, the coins go to your local bank!

Your children's eyes may start to glass over with this explanation, so show them a video to bring the whole process to life. An entertaining video on the making of coins is on The US Mint for Kids site at https://www.usmint.gov/learn/kids/about-us. This video is easy to understand and is interesting for parents as well.

THE MAKING OF A DOLLAR BILL

Dollar bill creation has some similarities as coins. US paper money is made by the Bureau of Engraving and Printing. There are two locations, one in Washington, DC, and the other in Fort Worth, Texas. Dollar bills are printed on special paper that is 75% cotton and 25% linen, created for more durability.

- • *Step 1—Design.* New bills are designed by artists at the Bureau of Engraving and Printing. They add anticounterfeit images into the design that will prevent people from being able to copy the bill.
- • *Step 2—Engraving.* The image of the dollar bill is engraved onto giant steel plates.
- • *Step 3—Manufacturing.*
  - ◦ Ink is spread on the printing plates and then wiped off so that ink remains in only the grooves of the plates. Just like a huge stamp.
  - ◦ The plates are then pressed into the special blended paper with about 20 tons of pressure.
  - ◦ *Inspection.* Each sheet is analyzed to make sure that the paper, ink, and printing all meet the exact standards.
  - ◦ *Stacking and cutting.* Here, the sheets are stacked and sent to a large cutting machine that slices the sheets into individual bills. Now, the bills are considered legal money. After cutting, the bills are sent out to the banks.

Sharing Fun Facts about Money[2]

- • A penny costs 2.4 cents to manufacture.
- • More than 2 million Americans live on less than $2 a day.

- It takes around 8,000 folds before a bill will tear from use.
- There is more Monopoly money printed every year than actual cash.
- The largest denomination of US currency was the $100,000 bill.

MONEY FROM OTHER COUNTRIES

Explain to your children that although they've learned so much about money, this chapter was just about money in the United States. Different countries have different kinds of money, called *currency*. Tell your children that this is because each country has its own policies and rules. For example, Mexico's currency is called the peso, and many European countries use the euro.

BOOKS FOR LEARNING

- *Bunny Money* by Rosemary Wells. A sweet book about a bunny named Ruby who has money to buy her grandma a present. Throughout the day she continues to have to use her money for other things and is worried she won't have enough left for the gift. This is a great book at this point to introduce younger kids to the concept of money and make it relevant to them.
- *The Penny Pot* by Stuart J. Murphy. Provides an entertaining and straightforward way to teach children about money and counting by actually counting coins throughout the book. Naturally, this book is great for helping children with their math skills as well.
- *A Dollar, a Penny, How Much and How Many?* by Lerner Publications. A basic explanation of coins and dollars and the value of each. The rhyming throughout helps keep the little ones engaged.
- *Counting with Common Cents* series by Deirdre McCarthy. Simple and beautifully illustrated books about money in the most basic forms. Each book provides a fun journey with adorable characters that will grab your young children's attention.
- *Follow the Money* by Loreen Leedy. Follow George, a newly minted quarter, on his way to the bank. All day he is traded, spent, lost, found, donated, dropped into a vending machine, washed in a washing machine, and generally passed all around town.

ONLINE RESOURCES

- *Counting Money app*. This is an easy-to-use app to help kids learn their coins and help with counting. It's interactive and engaging,

featuring true or false, memory, and other simple and fun games. Costs $2 to download.
https://itunes.apple.com/us/app/counting-money/id469420537?mt=8

- *Money Professor app.* This is another simple app for the younger kids, which includes matching games, "which is greater?," and counting activities. A virtual piggy bank allows kids to keep track of how much they "win" and buy prizes with their winnings. Costs $1 to download. https://itunes.apple.com/us/app/money-professor-a-money-counting-game/id1096417859?mt=8
- *Count Money! app.* For those parents looking for a free app, this one does exactly what the title says: Count Money! It's simple, but great for parents helping younger kids refine their skills.
https://itunes.apple.com/us/app/count-money/id517571875?mt=8
- *US Mint for Kids* site is an extensive resource for children learning about money and includes fun games and activities for all ages. https://www.usmint.gov/learn/kids
- *Kidsmathgamesonline.com* has a slightly addicting simple counting game for kids.
http://www.kidsmathgamesonline.com/money/moneycounting.html

SHORT AND SWEET TAKEAWAYS

1. Let your children interact with coins and cash frequently, whether it's sorting, counting, stacking, or simply observing.
2. Money provides a perfect opportunity to work on your children's counting skills! Have them count up different amounts and ask them to come up with different coin combinations to get to a specific amount.
3. Play board games like Monopoly and Game of Life to teach your children how to manage money firsthand (and have some family fun).
4. Money does not grow on trees. There are a lot of steps, materials, and people involved to perfectly create the money we use every day.

NOTES

1. Folger, Jean. n.d. "Teaching Financial Literacy to Kids: What Is Money?" Accessed September 3, 2018. https://www.investopedia.com/university/teaching-financial-literacy-kids/teaching-financial-literacy-kids-what-money.asp.
2. Leonhardi, Jennifer. 2018. "20 Weird Facts About Money Most Of Us Don't Know." Supermoney, April 21, 2018. https://www.supermoney.com/2014/08/20-absurd-facts-about-money/.

4

Why Do We Need Money?

Even adults can lose sight of why we really need money. We know we need money, we want money . . . but what is the real purpose of it? Money is simply a piece of green paper, yet it is the most reported on and talked about subject out there. Who has money, who doesn't have money, lifestyles of the rich and famous, how to make more money, how to spend less money, greed . . . the list goes on and on.

Within all of this chatter, there are such conflicting messages about money. On the one hand, many envy the wealthy and spend their life wanting more money. On the other hand, you often hear things like "money is the source of all evil" and wanting more money is greedy.

One of the primary goals of this chapter is to start kids off with a positive attitude around money. Again, money is simply a tool that can be used to reach our goals. It's easy to lose sight of this and a good reminder for everyone, not just parents teaching children. Children absorb so much of what they hear and are so easily influenced, especially at this young age. If their first experiences with money are hearing their parents idolizing the wealthy or blaming money for their problems, their own attitudes will become shaped with similar beliefs. Children should understand that, while money is not everything, it is still extremely important.

WHAT IS MONEY, REALLY?

To begin explaining the importance of money, be sure your children understand at a very basic level the following three points:

1. *Money is used to buy things.* By elementary school most kids probably have this one down cold ("Can you buy me some ice cream?"). They should also understand that some things cost a lot of money, like a house, and some things cost less money, like a popsicle. While that's an obvious example, some are not so simple and depend on the value and cost of an item.
2. *Money doesn't grow on trees.* Although we all swear we won't say the things our parents said to us, most parents probably have heard themselves say this one to their children. Kids should know that you have to work to make money; it doesn't just magically appear. More on working in Chapter 5.
3. *You can't buy everything.* There is only a certain amount of money, so you have to choose what you buy. If you buy one thing, it means you can't use that money to buy something else (opportunity cost, discussed later). This is the hardest one for kids to grasp but one of the more important concepts in economics.

Anytime Activity: How Does Our Family Use Money?

Start the conversation close to home. Ask your children why they think we need money. The younger children may stick with answers like to buy toys, to get food at the grocery store, and to go to the movies. Older children may mention home payments, electricity, and college (if any children answer retirement, you get a gold star for parenting . . . this is not usually on their radar yet!). Regardless of their answer, talk through each one: "That's exactly right. If we want a banana, we need to go to a store and give them money. In exchange, they give us a banana. So, when we're hungry, we need money to buy food."

Once they've exhausted their own list, walk through your day and brainstorm with them different ways your family interacted with money today. It's not just for fun or food; money is used in ways that they may not realize. Examples could be:

- *We turned on the lights in our bedrooms.* "Lights use electricity, and we pay the power company every month for all the electricity we used."
- *Mom made coffee.* "I used money to buy the coffee from the store. Also, everything that's plugged in uses electricity, and we pay for electricity."
- *We all got dressed.* "I bought your shirt at the mall last week."
- *Dad drove the kids to school.* "I had to buy a car from a car dealership. Plus, cars need gas to run, so I spend money on gas."
- *Mom went to work.* "I get paid for working, and I work so that our family has money for food, car, and gas."

- *Their babysitter met them at the bus stop.* "Mom and Dad pay money to someone to take care of you so that we can make money for the family. Your babysitter then uses that money for her own food and gas."
- *They went to their friends' house after homework to play.* "Your friends' parents have to spend money every month to pay for their house."
- *We packed for our vacation.* "We don't just use money for things we need. We also can use money for fun extra things, like going on trips."

Clearly, these conversations can get complex very quickly. It's fine if your children are young and don't completely grasp how you pay for your house. At that point it can just be an introduction so they start to think about how your family uses money. However, if your children ask lots of questions and the answers get more and more complicated—that's fantastic! That just means they are thinking and interested in the subject.

WHY IS MONEY IMPORTANT?

Once you've discussed how money is used in everyday life, your children can now start to see the bigger picture on why money is important.

- *Money buys the things you need to live.* "You have to have money to buy a house, clothes to wear, and food to eat."
- *Money provides protection.* "If you're hurt, we can pay for you to go to the hospital and get better."
- *Money gives you choices.* "I make enough money in my day job that I don't have to work at nights and can come home to my family" or "We have enough money saved that I can stay home and raise my kids."
- *Money allows you to have a more comfortable life.* "Money allows us to buy and do special extra things, like take our family trip to the beach or have a house with a nice yard."
- *Money allows you to help other people and the community.* "We can buy toys or clothes to give to children who don't have any, or we can donate money to the animal shelter to help sick dogs."
- *Money allows parents to provide the best for their children.* "We work hard so we have enough money to send you to college. If you have a college education, you can get a better job when you get older."
- *Money means less worry.* "Of course, everyone worries about something, but there are people who don't have enough money to buy food for their family or buy a house to live in. They feel constant worry and stress."

WHAT DOES IT COST?

Your children have probably heard you say that something is too expensive to buy, but what does that mean to them? To start teaching your children about prices, start simply and tell them what things cost as you're shopping. Children are naturally curious and will ask you if that's a lot of money or why it costs more than other items.

Explain that the company selling the good or service sets the price and it's based on how important it is to a customer and how much it costs the company to make it. In the beginning they won't have a basis of comparison, so when you tell them something costs $100, they'll have no idea if that's high or low. But as you go, they will start to see that some items cost more than others. This will lead into conversations like "Why are these two watches that look the same different prices?" and "Why does a car cost more than a bike?"

Real-World Activity: Grocery Store Guessing Game

Next time you are in the grocery store cashier line with your children, take turns guessing the total cost of your food. Help them guess by estimating the cost of individual items. Whoever is the closest gets a prize (or a simple high-five could work too). This activity has the added bonus of distracting your children from the rows of candy conveniently placed at the check-out.

SHORT AND SWEET TAKEAWAYS

1. To show children the importance of money, illustrate throughout the day how your family uses money, such as by buying food, using electricity, and driving a car.
2. Money is not just important for buying things. Talk to your children about the broader uses of money. It provides protection, gives us choices, and can help others.

5

How Do We Get Money?

Now that your children are starting to grasp how important money is, they may be asking you "How do I get some?" The goal of Chapter 5 is to teach children some of the many different ways that money can be earned. This can be fun for children because you can start conversations about their passions and show them how they can turn them into a career when they get older. Earning money will later be applied to real life in Chapter 7, which is all about the infamous allowance and how parents can best use it to teach children about earning money.

WHAT IS A JOB?

To begin teaching young children about how we get money, they first need to understand the concept of working and jobs. Most children have heard their parents say a hundred times, "Not now, Mom's working" or "Daddy has to go into the office to work." So your children know that you work, but do they know what work is? Some may have an idea, but it may seem like a mythical concept to them. Do they understand that parents work to make money? Maybe not.

Tell your children a job is the work that someone does to earn money. The easiest way to teach children how we get money is through your own personal examples. Ask your children what they think you do for work. It can be eye opening and entertaining to see how your children perceive what you do. A past *Tonight Show* episode featured "Take Your Parents to Work Day" (https://www.youtube.com/watch?v=c5UBvzrBb_c), where host Jimmy Fallon asks young children what they think their parents actually do at work all day. The answers ranged from "He sits at a computer" to "I have no idea" and "She works, then gets grumpy!"

Parents may need to start at the beginning with the younger children. Whatever they tell you that they think you do, first point out the parts that are true. "Yes, that's right, part of what I do at work is I sit at a computer." Then, help them fill in the gaps by providing very broad descriptions of your job. Some are easier than others—like teachers, firefighters, and doctors—because your children already have experience with them.

Regardless of your occupation, think of one simple line that describes your job. Then, give them a few examples of things you do every day, what you like about it, and what you don't like. Make it relevant to them. If you work for a media company, bring home a copy of the magazine. If you work for a company that makes office products, bring an example home.

Next, try to show them the bigger picture about what you do. Why do you do it? Why does your company or industry exist? For example, if you work in real estate, the purpose of your job is to help people find a home to live in. Explain why that's important. Tell them something about your job that you are passionate about, like helping people, adventure, working outside, or creating things. The reason you work is to make money, but children should understand that work can (and should) be fun, inspiring, important, and interesting.

Make this an ongoing conversation with your children. Obviously, you don't want to tell them how dumb one of your clients is or how your boss doesn't know what he's doing. Keep it positive and try to engage your children in your day by telling them something funny that happened at work or, when they are talking about their school day, add in a relevant story from your workday.

Finally, if you can, bring your children to work with you every once in a while. Show them where you sit, the people you talk to, and some of the things you do every day. Now, they can visualize it when you talk about your workday.

Anytime Activities: Jobs Are All Around Us

There are opportunities every day to incorporate careers and jobs into conversations with your kids. Not all need to be lengthy, sit-down discussions. Point out different career examples throughout your daily lives so your children will continue to grow their understanding of what working means. Below are several examples:

- When talking about friends and family members, talk about what they do for work. If your children have questions or seem interested in something specific, encourage them to ask those friends and family members directly. Same goes for the people they come into contact with each day, including bus drivers, doctors, and teachers. Don't forget to give those people a heads-up that they are about to get a third-degree interrogation from your children so they know it's coming.

- Talk about things your children love to do or care about and how they can make it their job when they get older. These conversations shouldn't feel pressured to the children. Just simply make them aware that, when they are older, they can turn their passions into jobs. If your children love to paint, tell them about famous artists, or bring them to a local museum.
- TV shows can provide an opportunity to point out careers that your children may not come into contact with every day, like an astronaut, scientist, or judge.

Pretend Play: Go to Work

List several jobs and ask your children to pick one that they want to have. Use jobs that they are already familiar with through their own experiences, like teacher, coach, doctor, or veterinarian. Help them set up shop and brainstorm with them everything that they do as part of their job.

Explain to them how they will make money from this job. If they are vets, they will get paid each time a patient comes to see them. If they are teachers, they will get paid every other week by their boss. Get pretend money and make it a part of the experience. If your children are vets, set up their office, roleplay, and bring in multiple (stuffed) animals with varying afflictions. Make this fun, and let your children's imagination run wild.

Discussion

Talk about what parts your children liked and didn't like about the jobs. Also, ask them what some other ways are that they could have made money. If they were vets, maybe they could have also sold health products for dogs. Finally, ask them details about their jobs. Did they work indoors or outdoors? Did they work for themselves or big companies? This leads to the conversation of the different types of jobs.

TYPES OF JOBS

As your children can imagine, jobs come in all shapes and colors. Some people love computer work, and some want to interact more with other people. This is important for kids to understand so they know they have choices when they get older. You will notice their wheels start to spin about what type of job may work best for them based on their personality and interests. Keep the conversations fun and light; the purpose is to just get them thinking. Below are several examples you can provide to your children about the types of jobs out there.

- *Size of organization.* Tell your children they could work for a company like Disney that has thousands of other people working there or they could work for a small art studio with just a few people in the whole company.
- *Service or good.* As discussed more later in Chapter 11 (Kiddie Economics), they may be in a job that makes shoes (provides a good) or in a job that provides research on health (provides service).
- *Job location.* Their job could be in an office working on a computer, or they could work in the jungle studying monkeys. (Parents, be prepared with an answer when your children yell out, "I want to live in the jungle and study monkeys!")
- *Money.* Some jobs pay more money than other jobs. The reasons vary, based on the type of work, the company, the education required, and experience level. While money is important, and certainly a factor in what job one chooses, it should not be the only factor considered.

WHAT'S A BOSS?

One of the biggest differentiators in a type of job is whether they work for themselves or for someone else. Tell your children that, when they get older, they have a choice of who they work for and there are good parts and bad parts to each:

- *Working for yourself.* This is similar to having a lemonade stand, usually referred to as being an entrepreneur. As their own boss, your children get to do everything exactly how they want to do it. They make all the rules, make their own schedule, and can let their creativity fly. They also get to keep more of the money they make.
- *Working for someone else.* When they work for someone else, they don't have to be the boss, which can mean less pressure. They also have steady money, security, and consistency in their job. Additionally, people like working for other people because of the social aspect of it.

Tell your children that there is no right or wrong choice. But make sure they begin to understand their options so when they get older they make the choice that's best for them.

BOOKS FOR LEARNING

- *Clothesline Clues to Jobs People Do* by Kathryn Heling and Deborah Hembrook. This is a cute starter book for the younger kids, where they guess what someone's job is based on what he or she wears.
- *The Jobs People Do* book series by Linda Hayward. The books in this series provide a great way to illustrate specific jobs to children and what they do day to day. Examples in this series are *A Day in the Life of a Builder* and *A Day in the Life of a Firefighter*.

ONLINE RESOURCES

- *Careeronestop.org.* Do your children want to learn more about the field of architecture? What about sports training or agriculture? This is literally a one-stop shop, with simple videos and information explaining every field imaginable.
www.careeronestop.com
- *Knowitall.org.* Its Kids Work! Program is a virtual community of workplaces designed to give students an interactive job exploration experience that connects schoolwork to real work.
www.knowitall.org
- *NASA Kids Club.* What kid hasn't thought about being an astronaut? NASA does a great job of explaining what it does and why it's so important through games and online activities.
https://www.nasa.gov/kidsclub/index.html#.VIWzXzHF-So
- *Code.org.* Its stated mission is to grow computer science learning, which is valuable in so many fields. Elementary kids can learn to make their own game, app, or computer drawing.
www.code.org
- *KineticCity.com.* Encourage your budding scientists through this site, which uses science projects, experiments, and educational games, including activities that pull the young scientist away from the screen.
www.kineticcity.com
- *USA Government.* The US government has a site dedicated to teaching children about different jobs. From dog trainer to army dentist, it provides videos and resources on multiple professions that kids may enjoy learning about.
https://www.usa.gov/government-jobs-lesson-plan

SHORT AND SWEET TAKEAWAYS

1. Explain to your children that people work to make money. Start discussing with them what you do for work and what you like and dislike about it. You can use the people you come in contact with every day to teach your children about other types of jobs, like friends, bus drivers, doctors, and teachers.
2. There are thousands of ways to make money, and jobs come in all shapes and sizes. The most important point for your children is they can find a job that fits their personality and needs.

6

The Building Blocks
for Piggy Banks

Your children are probably close to the age (if not already there) where
they want you to "Show them the money!" Some of their friends may
have allowances and may boast at recess about how they are saving for a
new K'NEX set with their own money (because don't all kids boast about
their saving achievements?).

They are *so* close to getting their hands on some real money. But first,
for your children to learn to spend responsibly and understand the importance of saving and sharing, they need to learn some simple skills,
such as prioritizing what they spend money on and differentiating needs
from wants. Chapter 6 will also provide a blueprint for teaching your
children how to make smart decisions. This will all lead to Part III, which
will teach your children to apply these skills through spending, saving,
and sharing—the *Piggy Bank Basics.*

BUILDING BLOCK 1: NEEDS VERSUS WANTS

For the younger children, the first concept to teach them is the difference
between needs and wants. This concept seems pretty straightforward, but
it's not always clear cut. Water is clearly a need, but what about juice? If
they have a good grasp on the difference between the two, they can get
into the habit at a young age of asking themselves, "Do I really need this,
or do I just want it?" This is a valuable skill and can curb impulse buys
and overspending.

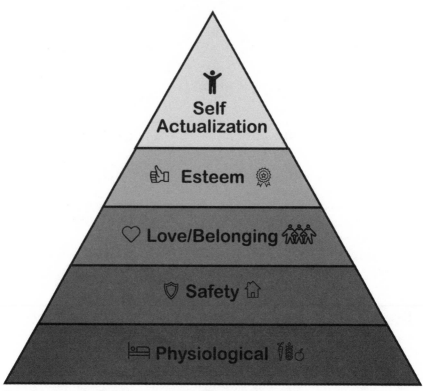

Figure 6.1.   Maslow's Hierarchy of Needs. *Kristen Buchholz.*

A quick review of needs versus wants will take you back to your Psych 101 college class, with *Maslow's hierarchy of needs*, illustrated in Figure 6.1. This pyramid demonstrates Maslow's theory by showing the five basic levels of human needs. You may be saying to yourself, "I understand the difference between wants and needs, thank you very much." However, when your eight-year-old future interrogator starts grilling you, this can be a helpful guide. You'll be surprised how quickly this can get tricky.

While not perfect, all five levels of need are important, and the theory gives parents a foundation for teaching. With regard to finance and explaining to your children the meaning of a *need*, focus on the first two levels: physiological and safety. *Physiological needs* are the physical requirements for your body to survive, such as water, food, shelter, and clothing. The next level isn't always as black and white. It focuses on what a human needs to be safe, such as savings accounts, safety in the home, health care, and job security. The top three levels are important but not as clear cut when explaining needs and wants to children—better to stick with the bottom two for now.

Your children probably have an idea of what wants and needs mean, but it's the kids' version. So it sounds something like "I need ice cream" and "I want water." To start with your children, ask them what babies need every day. They will probably answer with things like milk, mommy, toys, sleep, and a bed. With each item they list, explain whether that's something they *need* or something they *want*. "Toys are fun for babies, and they like to play with them. But they can live without toys." Next, ask your children what they need every day. Repeat the same activity as you did with the baby.

Now that they have an idea of wants versus needs with regard to their own lives, you can dig into what it really means. Simply put, *needs* are things that are essential, or important to your survival. *Wants* are things that are nice to have, but you can live without. Even still, this can get murky. You will have to determine for your family what is considered a need versus a want on some items, like a car. For many, a car is considered a need that is necessary to go to the grocery store, doctor's office, and school. For others, a car may be a luxury item that they cannot afford.

Along the same lines, while a car may be a need for some, a *luxury* car with all the bells and whistles is not. That would more likely be considered a want instead of a need. Food is a need, but ice cream is not. "But ice cream *is* a food!" your too-smart-for-their-own-good children will argue. You can explain to them that food is a need because it gives your body vital nutrients. Although ice cream is a food, it doesn't give your body those same nutrients. Then, you'll probably have to take a trip to the ice cream store since it was brought up. Sorry.

This leads to setting some financial expectations about what you expect your children to buy with their own money. Tell your children that while they are young, you will always buy them anything that is a *need*, such as food, their home, and clothes, but they have to buy the things they want with their own money (except for special occasions, of course). You can use opportunities at the grocery store as examples. If they ask for a certain type of cereal, tell them that's a need, so you will buy it for them. If they ask for a cake pop from the bakery, that would be considered a want.

This understanding of needs versus wants is a major building block in terms of learning smart spending. It will become critical once they start learning about budgets and making decisions on how to spend their hard-earned money. They should understand that while it's OK to spend money on things you want, need items should always come first.

Anytime Activities: Need versus Want

- Give your children the choice between two items and tell them to decide which is a need and which is a want. Start simple, like "bread and baby doll." Once they've got the basics, try to trick them with items like "shoes and barrettes," "Band-Aids and popsicle," and "house and beach house." It's not always as clear cut as you'd think, right? When the questions get trickier, ask them which one is *more* of a need than the other.

- Do the same game, but reverse the roles. Have your children name two items and you have to tell them which you think is a need and which is a want. It's interesting to see how they choose which is which.
- Ask your children to list needs and wants that don't cost any money. The obvious free needs are air and water. Ask for examples of what they could use to fulfill their needs while camping. If they needed shelter, they could build a fort for free with trees and branches. They could eat certain types of berries from the bushes. Examples of free wants are easier to come up with, like swimming in the lake, playing at the park, or exploring the woods.

Discussion

Keep this conversation going. It's amazing how kids absorb this type of information. But beware; your children are guaranteed to use this against you the next time you say, "I really need a bigger yard" by replying, "Mom, you don't need it. You just want it." Right, thanks, kid.

Practice Activity: At the Store

The thought of being at the store with your children usually conjures up some combination of fear and dread with most parents (for good reason: "I want this!" "I'm bored" "Another store? Ughhhhh!"). Unfortunately, learning firsthand from you is the most effective way for children to learn anything. So take your kids to run errands with you! What better way to teach children about spending than to show them how you spend? Any type of store will do, as long as you are buying a product or service in exchange for money.

Point out products on the shelves and ask if they are needs or wants. You can do the same at a service-oriented business, like a laundromat. "Is getting my clothes cleaned at a laundromat a need or a want?" Each time something falls into the gray area, you have a great opportunity to explain the concept further. "Washing my clothes is a need. But I *could* do it myself for less money. So paying extra to have someone else wash them is a *want*." Again, try to trip them up with these; don't make it too easy!

HOUSEHOLD AND FAMILY NEEDS

Once your children have a firm grasp on the difference between needs and wants, you can dive into the needs that are critical (but not as obvious) to running a household and family. To start with, power for your house is a good example:

- Ask your children if you need your oven? You can explain that the answer is yes because you need it to cook food.
- Ask your children if you need electricity/lights? The answer is yes for safety reasons. You need heat in the winter and air-conditioning in the summer. Plus, you need lights because you could trip and hurt yourself at night if it's too dark.
- Explain to them that power runs the oven, keeps the lights on, and heats the house up during the winter. Therefore, power is a need.
- Walk through the rest of your household bills as examples for your kids. Cable and internet are great examples to discuss. These probably *feel* like needs to most kids (and many adults!), so it's important to explain that these are most likely want items (unless you use it for work, then it could be considered a need). These conversations with your kids not only help differentiate between needs and wants, but discussing household bills introduces important items to be discussed later when exploring budgets.

BUILDING BLOCK 2: PRIORITIES

Through learning needs versus wants, your children have been learning how to prioritize, even if they don't know what this word means. A simple way to explain priorities to your children is to ask them what is really important to them. Maybe you are one of the lucky and rare parents where your children will tell you that their family is most important. More than likely, they list things like their friend Sam, their bike, frogs, or cupcakes. Tell them that these are their *priorities*, which means these are the things that are most important to them. Explain to them that a need is always more important than a want, so it's a *priority*.

Practice Activity: Prioritizing

Write a list of 10 items unique to your children, including a mix of things they like and dislike. Ask them to rank the items in importance from 1–10

Table 6.1.   Rank Priorities

Rank (1–10)	Priority
	The Incredibles 2
	Pickles
	Ninjago LEGO Set
	Mom
	Cleaning your room
	Fudge brownies
	Baby brother
	Sleep
	Math homework
	Spaceships

(with 1 being the most important and 10 being the least important). Make it fun, creative, and challenging. Include items whose rankings may surprise you . . . such as their baby brother.

This should be something that initiates lively discussions as your children decide what they like most, and you will probably learn something new about your children (such as, Does Mom rank above brownies?). Table 6.1 provides an example list. Walk through the list and explain to them that #1 is more important than #2, so it's more of a priority and so on down the list.

BUILDING BLOCK 3: DECISION-MAKING

Psychology expert Jim Taylor states that decision-making is one of the most important skills children need to develop to become healthy and mature adults. In the article "Parenting: Decision Making," Taylor explains why.

> Decision making is crucial because the decisions your children make dictate the path that their lives take. Teaching your children to make their own decisions has several benefits. When they make a good decision, they can gain the greatest amount of satisfaction and fulfillment because they chose it. When your children make bad decisions, they may suffer for it, but they can learn from the experience and make better decisions in the future.[1]

Responsible spending stems from smart decision-making. However, it's important for your children to learn how to make not only smart financial decisions but also good decisions regarding health, education, safety, and general well-being. Although this chapter focuses on financial decisions, the lessons and information can be applied to any type of decision your children face.

Right or wrong, your children are already experienced decision-makers. Decision-making is a skill your children use all day long. Many of their decisions are small and set on autopilot, like deciding to put their shoes on in the morning. Others are larger decisions and may require some thought, like which friend to play with at recess. Start pointing out when your children are making a decision or compliment them when they make a well thought out decision, even if it's small.

Explain to your children that they make decisions all the time, and often their decision means they are choosing one thing instead of another. When they decide they want vanilla ice cream that means they're deciding to eat that flavor instead of the chocolate ice cream. Same with spending. When you spend your money on one item, it means you can't buy something else with that money—it's all about choices.

This is an example of *opportunity cost*: giving up the benefit of one thing for another (more in Chapter 11). If your children choose vanilla ice cream, the opportunity cost is that they can't have chocolate ice cream. If your children have two birthday parties at the same time and they choose to go to Josh's party instead of Megan's party, the opportunity cost is they miss Megan's party.

STEPS TO SMART DECISION-MAKING

Let's look at an example that every parent (unfortunately) knows all too well. You are with your children at the local carnival, mall, fair, or amusement park. Your children have some money from their allowances burning a hole in their pockets. The first toy they see is a cheaply made, knock-off stuffed Minion doll (insert latest movie character here), which they decide they *must* have. Every urge in your parent body is screaming to tell them not to buy it because you know in 20 minutes it will either fall apart or they will find something else they want. However, this is a perfect time to let your children make their own decision and help guide them through the decision-making process. These steps can be applied to a financial decision like this or any other situation your children are in.

1. *Stop and identify the decision.* Because your children are young, they are naturally impulsive and often jump at their first whim. Your children may not even realize they are making a decision. So the first step is to encourage your children to slow down and recognize that there is a decision that needs to be made.

Minion example: "OK, Bella, I understand that you really want this doll. Before you make the decision to buy this doll, let's stop and think about it for a minute, just to make sure you'll be happy with your decision."

If you immediately tell her she shouldn't get the doll, it makes her defenses rise, meaning she will now insist on getting the horrid doll. By acknowledging that she has a decision to make, it not only slows her down but also lets her know that this is *her* decision and gives her a feeling of control.

2. *List the options.* Make sure your children understand that any time they make a decision, they are choosing one option over the others. Ask your children what their options are and discuss the possible opportunity costs.

   Minion example: Ask Bella what her choices are in this decision. She may say, "I can buy this Minion doll, or I can buy a different toy." Help her see that there may be other options, such as saving her money for something later. Another option could be waiting a day, and if she still really wants it (she won't), she can then come back and buy it. The opportunity cost for buying the Minion is she can't buy another toy or save that money.

3. *Evaluate your options.* Walk your children through the pros and cons of each option. This is the time to ask questions, such as "Why do you want this?" and "What are you going to do with it?"

   Minion example: "Bella, it seems like your options are to (1) buy this doll now, (2) wait a day before buying it, (3) find another toy to buy now, or (4) save your money for later. Let's think about each option. If you buy it now, you could have a lot of fun playing with it, but how will you feel if it falls apart tomorrow? Or if you buy it now, will you be upset if there's something you want more when we go to the Disney store tomorrow, but you already spent all your money? What will happen if we wait and walk around a little? We can always come back if you still want it."

   Clearly every parent reading this is trying to gently guide her children away from the hypnotic Minion, but be sure to make it known that this is *their* decision.

4. *Make your choice, then analyze.* Ask your children what their decision is. Then, bite your tongue and roll with it. Note that obviously "rolling with it" may not always be appropriate. Children don't have the maturity and experience to make important decisions. If it's a large decision or one with real consequences (such as buying a dangerous toy or choosing a sleepaway camp), parents may need to step in to decide for the children. However, if it's a decision where the worst-case consequences don't harm your children (or others), then just let them choose. Letting them fail and feel the disappointment of a

wrong decision will encourage them to avoid bad decisions in the future. Later, discuss with your children if they are happy with their decision and what they wished they had done differently.

> *Minion example:* After all of this, Bella decides to get the wretched doll. Even though you are screaming inside, let her make the mistake. If you tell her she will regret it, you will most likely get either an eye roll or an emphatic "No, I love Minions, I will play with this *all* the time!" The only way she will learn is to go ahead and buy the doll and realize on her own that she made a mistake.
>
> When she inevitably regrets this decision, avoid the temptation to tell her that you knew she would. Ask her why she regrets the decision and what she wishes she had done. Try to get to the root of why she regrets her purchase. Is it because the toy is falling apart? If so, talk to her about the importance of quality, and suggest she study a toy carefully first to make sure it won't break. Maybe she regrets it because after walking around the carnival, she found a toy she wanted more than the Minion. If that's the case, tell her that the next time she wants something, it's OK to wait and make sure that's what she really wants to spend her money on. When she breaks down crying because she "really, really" wants this new toy and "life is so unfair," give her a big hug and say "I know sweetie. I'm sorry you're sad." Offer her a tissue and stand your ground.

Depending on type and size of the decision, the decision process could take a total of two minutes or two weeks. More than likely, your children are already conducting some version of this process with every decision. However, it probably goes something like "I want that Minion doll. I can buy this Minion doll now. I'm going to buy the Minion doll. Mom, the eye fell off! I wish I hadn't bought this stupid Minion doll." All you need to do is help them stretch out the process and think it through.

Discussion

Whether they are happy with their ultimate decision or regret the purchase, talk to them about what they did well and what they could have done differently. Now that they have some distance, they may be able to realize that they didn't really want the Minion doll and try to understand why they bought it in the first place.

Practice Activity: Making Decisions

The best way to teach children to make good decisions is through practice. Let them make their own decisions early and often. Again, allow them to make mistakes because that's how they will learn.

Sorry, parents, but once again running errands provides a great opportunity to teach. At the store, give your children $5 and tell them they can buy something. Help them walk through the decision-making process. A note to parents: be sure to carve out a few extra minutes with this one. All parents have experienced the hour-long process of choosing between a pink or blue lollipop . . . just imagine what they can do with $5.

Also, try to give them clear choices throughout the day so they can practice making decisions, and encourage them to go through the process even on simple decisions.

- Do you want ice cream or a popsicle?
- Do you want to do your homework now and get it over with or wait until later?
- Would you like to decide what to wear to school today, or should I pick out your outfit?
- Whose birthday party do you want to go to this Saturday?

Since your children learn best watching you, discuss your own personal decisions throughout the day. If it's a decision you've already made, explain to them how you made it and how you feel about the decision. Ask them what they think about your decision. Or, if you are struggling with a decision, explain the situation to your children and ask them for help.

Anytime Activity: "Would You Rather?"

Would you rather? is an easy way to let your children practice decision-making through hypotheticals and games. Come up with scenarios to propose to your children and have them decide what they would do. These can be financially motivated, based on simple everyday decisions, or important decisions, such as ones that deal with peer pressure. Then, switch roles, and have your children ask the questions.

These can be simple or complex and have more than one choice and not all need to have right or wrong answers. The purpose of these is to help your children identify when they are making a decision and think through the decision-making process. They also may get creative with their answers! Ask them why they chose the way they did so they are actually thinking through their answers. Children love these types of games because they have their parents' undivided attention . . . and it's all about them! Here are some examples:

- Would you rather be a dolphin or a tiger?
- Would you rather go to a party with all of your friends or spend the day with your best friend?

- Would you rather be able to fly or become invisible?
- Would you rather have 100 quarters or 30 one-dollar bills?
- You're at the ice cream store, and there are only two treats left: a quadruple scoop of plain vanilla ice cream with no toppings *or* a tiny scoop of vanilla with sprinkles and hot fudge. Which would you rather eat?
- You are at your friend Jenny's house with your friends Sarah and Ella. They decide that once Jenny's parents go to sleep they are going to sneak outside to swim in the pool by themselves. Your mom told you that you are not allowed to swim in the pool without an adult because it's too dangerous. Your friends all decide to do it. Would you rather go swimming with them or stay inside?
- You are at the toy store with Mom, and she gives you $10 to spend on whatever you want. She tells you that if you don't spend it and wait until tomorrow, you guys can come back to the toy store and she'll give you another $10. Which would you rather do—buy something today or wait until you have more money?

BOOKS FOR LEARNING

Lily Learns About Wants and Needs by Lisa Bullard. This is a straightforward book perfect for the younger elementary school children. It shows Lily in multiple situations where she has to make decisions on spending money and teaches about wants versus needs.

MATCHING GAME: TERMS TO KNOW

Table 6.2. Matching Game: Terms to Know

Match each of these important terms to its correct definition.

Needs	The things that are nice to have, but you can live without.
Wants	The things that are most important.
Priorities	The things that are essential or important to your survival.

SHORT AND SWEET TAKEAWAYS

1. Explain to your children the difference between needs and wants. Make sure they understand that needs always come before wants.
2. Decision-making is one of the most important skills your children need to develop. Let them practice making decisions while they are young and can learn from their mistakes.

3. When your children are faced with a decision, guide them through the decision-making process; then, ultimately, let them have the final say.

NOTE

1. Taylor, Jim. 2009. "Parenting: Decision Making." *Psychology Today*, October 19, 2009. https://www.psychologytoday.com/us/blog/the-power-prime/200910/parenting-decision-making

Part III

PIGGY BANK BASICS (SAVE, SHARE, AND SPEND)

Intermediate Level: 1st–5th Grade

7

Allowance and Kid Jobs

Here it comes—the great allowance debate. The "right" way to give your kids an allowance has become a topic of conversation and source of stress for many parents. If you give your children an allowance for chores, does it teach them that they get paid for doing things they should already be doing? Will they become entitled? However, if you pay kids an allowance that's *not* tied to any work, will they become even more entitled by thinking they get money for free? Oh, and what about how much money to give them?

The sources of stress about allowance are endless, which makes sense because we're parents and stress is what we do best. However, this chapter will show you that there's very little proven "right" or "wrong" when giving your children an allowance. As long as you follow some basic ground rules and stay consistent, you (probably) won't completely ruin your children's money management skills for life.

HOW TO STRUCTURE ALLOWANCE

There are two general schools of thought, both supported by different financial professionals.

1. *Tie allowance to chores.* It's simple: your children do chores, and they get paid. Not doing chores means no money. There are several positives to this approach. Your children learn early that they need to work to make money. It helps them make choices and learn

consequences. For example, if they choose not to do the dishes, they don't get the money to buy a new toy. This approach also provides children with the most important tool used to teach about money . . . which is money!

However, there are several negatives to this approach. It teaches children that they don't *have* to do chores, that chores are a choice. They also may be rewarded for doing things they should be doing anyway: making their beds, putting away their dishes, and cleaning up after themselves.

This leads to the question of deciding exactly what you pay them for and what they have to do. Do you pay them for putting their dishes in the sink? What about helping Dad rake the leaves? How will you answer when they say "I'll only do it if you pay me"?

Or what if your children decide they don't need money this week, so they refuse to do any chores? While the chore-based allowance has obvious value, there is a lot of gray area that is not addressed, and it's not always realistic for the real world.

2. *Give an allowance that's not tied to any chores.* With this approach, children get an allowance each week, no matter what. Separately, they are expected to do their chores and help around the house because they are part of the family. There is no link to allowance and work.

   What works well in this scenario is that no matter what, your children will have money. This is important because, for your children to really grasp money, they should have their own money to use. Another benefit is they learn that chores are something they are expected to do because it's their responsibility, not because they will get money. Critics of this approach believe that you're in danger of raising entitled children who believe that money will be handed to them and they won't learn the value of hard work.

ALLOWANCE HYBRID

With these options, what are parents to do? First, don't beat yourself up on this one. No matter what anyone says, there is no confirmed "right" way to give an allowance. It depends on the children, the family's finances, and your personal beliefs. As long as you aren't putting them in harm's way by forcing them to scale the roof for allowance or giving them enough for a down payment on a Porsche, you're probably not causing irreparable harm. You know your children. If one approach will clearly work better for your particular children, use that one.

However, if you are like most parents and not sure which to choose, the hybrid approach provides the best of both worlds. Give your children a set amount of money each week as allowance. This should not be tied to any chore or job. Separately, make it clear to them that, as part of the family, they are expected to do certain daily chores, like make their beds, put away their dishes, clean up their toys, and so on. Tell your children, if they want to earn *additional* money, they can do other jobs around the house. These jobs should be different from the daily chores they are expected to do. Some examples are washing windows, giving the dog a bath, washing your car, or raking the leaves.

The hybrid approach gives parents a real-world, enforceable way to give their children allowance. It removes the gray areas, sets clear expectations, and gives their children real money to learn from. When you are ready to start an allowance program with your children, be as clear as possible with your explanation.

> Josh, because you are getting older and there are things that you want to do and buy, I'm going to start giving you an *allowance*. That means, each week we will give you $6, which you can put in your piggy bank. Some of that money can be used to buy toys or games right away, and the rest will be saved for bigger items or shared with others.

Much more to come on that in the following chapters.

ALLOWANCE RULES

Regardless of the allowance method you use, keep the following points in mind.

- *Be consistent.* If you are planning to give your children a set amount of money each week, make sure you give it to them. If you identified certain extras that they can get paid for, make sure you pay them. Most importantly, don't pay for anything you identified as the chores that you expect your children to do.
- *Establish boundaries* on what they are expected to buy with their own money and what you will pay for. Kindergarten through 1st-grade children will still rely on their parents for most purchases, plus they won't have saved up enough to buy anything significant. At this younger age, tell your children that their allowance is for "extras" and define what those extras are. There's no right or wrong definition.

  The purpose is for them to start learning how to make smart choices with their money. For example, you can tell them their allowance is for things they may want to buy when running errands with their parents, treats at the local bakery, and bigger toys they want to save for.

As they get older, determine who pays for what by dividing everything into "needs and wants," which is discussed in more detail in the next chapter. Again, this is for the purpose of teaching, so the spectrum should be wide and flexible. Although new clothes for school may technically be a "want," they obviously shouldn't be expected to pay for them at this point. However, if they want a necklace to go with it, you could tell them that they need to use their allowance because it's a want.

Same can go for entertainment. At an amusement park, you could pay for a certain number of rides, but if they want that extra turn on the bumper cars, they need to pay for it. Again, no right or wrong answers here. The purpose is to teach them how to make decisions on spending money.

- *What's the amount?* How much money should you give your children? This is the million-dollar question. A 2018 survey from allowance tracker RoosterMoney found that the average kid between the ages of 4 and 14 takes home around $8.43 a week, with the amount increasing as they get older.[1] How much they get is up to the parents and depends on their personal financial situation.

  A solid rule of thumb is $1 for each year. So at five years old they get $5/week, at six years old they get $6/week, and so on. Just make sure you increase that amount as they get older. Their wants and needs get more expensive, and don't forget about inflation!

- *Cash is king.* Always give them allowance in cash and coins. One reason is so the children can continue to become familiar with tangible money, as discussed in Chapter 2. Also, children should be able to see their money grow, literally, in a piggy bank.

- *Allowance should be positive.* Don't use allowance as a punishment. If your children misbehave, don't tell them you'll take away their money that week. Allowance is most children's first hands-on experience with money; you don't want it to cause them anxiety. Besides, there are plenty of other ways to punish your children, by taking away privileges, electronics, and toys.

- *Manage expectations.* Remember the objective of allowance. You are not giving your children an allowance in the hopes that they'll be able to save enough for college. You are setting up a foundation for them to learn about money. They can use their allowance to practice spending, saving, giving, making mistakes, and learning smart decision-making. This is the time for them to learn, when there are no *real* consequences from bad decisions.

Real-World Activity: Collecting Bottles

Before sending your children out to the harsh, cruel real world of working (see below), start small. An easy way is by collecting bottles and cans and redeeming them for money. Have your children collect all the bottles from your house once a week (or they can even ask the neighbors). The containers that take the bottles can usually be found at grocery stores. They are not only earning money, but are also helping with chores, plus saving the environment. Not a lot of downside to this gem.

EARNING EXTRA MONEY

When your children are younger, around kindergarten through first grade, allowance and home chores will probably be the extent of their work experience. As your children get older, they may want to start looking at external ways to make money. Obviously, you are not going to submit an application for your third grader to wait tables at the local restaurant, but elementary school kids have plenty of opportunities to earn a little extra. Easiest way to do it? Have them start their own business!

The first question most parents have is "Should my children work?" It's a valid question, and it's not recommended (or legal!) to make your children get a "real" job until they're much older. "Working" is a loose term at this age and simply refers to an extracurricular activity that provides a fun experience and earns money.

BENEFITS OF WORKING

- *Provides an appreciation for the value of money.* If it takes them an hour of raking their neighbor's yard to earn $10, then that $10 is not just a magic piece of paper. It's worth an hour of their hard work.
- *Skin in the game.* Your children have no problem spending *your money* . . . but what if it's their hard-earned money? They may spend it a bit more carefully.
- *Teaches entrepreneurship.* Working teaches them about the opportunities available to them and provides real-life learnings on entrepreneurialism.
- *Learn about themselves.* What better way to learn what they like and don't like than by trying it out.
- *It plants an important seed within your children.* Working teaches responsibility and accountability at a young age, which are necessary traits to be a successful adult.

WORKING GUIDELINES

- *Start small.* Only you can determine what your children are ready for at their age. Any jobs they do at the elementary school level should be quick, safe, easy, and fun . . . and never forced on them.
- *Give them a choice and provide motivation.* If they want an American Girl doll that you aren't willing to buy for them, ask them if they want to earn extra money.
- *Make sure to prioritize.* School, friends, family, and extracurricular activities should come first to young children. Working is something they should do in their extra time.
- *Always remember the goal.* Working at this age isn't really about making money. It's about lessons, character, and building a foundation to learn finance. Actually, earning money is just a bonus—although don't tell your children that! To them, saving up money to buy their new Transformer is all the motivation they need.
- *Be involved.* Work at this age should be close to home and with people you know and trust. Especially at the younger ages, there must be adult supervision. For example, if your fourth-grade children are going to walk the neighbor's dog, go with them in the beginning to help them identify a walking route and get to know the dog. Safety always comes first.
- *Make it fun!* This should be a positive experience for your children, not something they dread or view as a punishment. Identify things they love to do and help them figure out how they could turn it into a "job." Ideas for fun jobs for kids are provided later.

FUN JOBS FOR KIDS AT ALL AGES

The important word here is "fun." You are teaching them responsibility just by having them work, so it's OK for the work to be enjoyable. They are more likely to do it without complaining if it doesn't feel like work . . . and, at the end of the day, isn't less complaining what all parents strive for? Below are ideas for your young children to earn some money, learn some important lessons, and have fun. The guidelines and steps that were listed previously can be applied to any of these options. Tell your children that by starting one of these businesses, they are now officially entrepreneurs.

- *Car wash.* Have your children and some of their neighborhood friends set up a car wash in your driveway or a safe spot near your house.

- *Lemonade/baked goods stand.* This can be any type of seasonally appropriate treat: hot chocolate for winter, cookies (anytime!), or drinks and popsicles on warm days.
- *Sell food.* Along the same lines, if your children love to cook, they can sell jams, sandwiches, soups, and so on to friends and neighbors.
- *Yard work.* Yard work is a great way for your children to spend a day outside and get some exercise. While a lawn mower is probably too much for your young children to handle, they can offer to help rake the neighbor's leaves, garden, or weed.
- *Dog walking/pet sitting.* This can be a fun activity for children who love animals; however, it obviously requires supervision from a parent when entering someone's home, especially with strange dogs. If you have a friend traveling who needs their cat fed or dog walked, just plan to bring your children over and stay there with them while they work.
- *House sitting.* Again, an activity that should be supervised by a parent, but when a friend or neighbor is out of town, your children can offer to water plants and pick up mail.
- *Childcare/parent's helper.* Babysitting is one of the first "jobs" many kids will have. At the elementary school age, they are probably too young to babysit alone; however, they can be a parent's helper. There are plenty of parents who are at home with kids, but need to get work done, do laundry, or (gasp!) just have a moment to themselves. These parents will pay to have your children come over while they are home to help with their kids. This can involve playing, reading, and some light supervision.
- *Party help.* Anyone who has recently been to a kid's birthday party knows that it is total chaos. Older kids can provide a huge help by helping manage the activities and crafts, help with the younger kids, and give out birthday cake.
- *Sell a product.* If your children's passion is making jewelry, they may love the idea of making and selling custom jewelry. Same thing with paintings, bookmarks, cross stitch, or any type of craft.
- *Family business.* Let them help with the family business. Whether it's your personal business or an aunt's business, help them find odd jobs like cleaning or filing.
- *Entrepreneurial pursuits.* Let them create their own business. Kids have an incredibly unique way of seeing the world and problem solving. Ask them what kind of business they want to start, based on what they love to do. You never know, maybe you have the next tech giant or world-renowned chef on your hands! Even if it's not something they will immediately make money from, always encourage

them to find new ways to follow their passions. Write a cookbook, create doll clothing, or start a band.

Real-World Activity: Start a Business

Even if your children are on the younger side, you can make this even more impactful by making it a real business. Get your children involved from the very beginning and let them make decisions on the business. The more involved they are, the more ownership they will take over the business . . . meaning they will be more engaged.

- *What's the business?* Sit down with your children and make a list of things they like to do. Use an idea from the list above or come up with a new idea. Of those, what could be turned into a service or product that they could offer to others? For example, if your children love dogs, they could offer a dog walking service. If they love gardening, they could help tend to a neighbor's garden while they are out of town. Another way to brainstorm jobs is to look at your household and identify areas where you could use help, such as getting your car washed, picking weeds in the garden, and painting the fence. Regardless of what business they choose, the process of starting is similar for each.
- *Prepare.* What do they need to prepare? If they are going to be a parent helper, they may need to get CPR and first aid training. What do they need to learn to make sure they are really good at the service they provide? If they are starting a car washing or yard work business, they will need to purchase materials. Brainstorm and create a checklist.
- *Pricing.* Decide how much they will charge. Parents can help with this by simply doing some market research: ask friends and neighbors what they would pay or what others charge. The structure will vary depending on the service. For example, providing dog washing will be a one-time fee, whereas pet sitting a dog while your neighbor is out of town would be based on the amount of time they are gone. Come up with several pricing scenarios and adjust as needed per service.
- *Accounting.* More details on accounting will be provided in Chapter 11, but for now parents can teach their children about basic business finance: revenue, costs of materials, and profits. List out everything it will cost to run this business: marketing materials, supplies, gas . . . brainstorm with your children anything you may need to buy. Then, determine how long until they "break even."

  For example, if they are starting a car washing business, they will need to buy washcloths, towels, soap, a hose, and a bucket. If their total supplies cost $50 and they charge $5 per wash, they will have to wash 10 cars to make their money back (Figure 11.2 in Chapter 11 shows a simple accounting worksheet). Once they reach the break-even point, any money they make is profit. At this age, it's probably best to let them keep all revenue. If they got to keep only their profits, it may actually discourage them from working!

- *Target market and safety.* Determine your target market. This is important for several reasons, and the adults must be involved. Most important is their safety; if they are walking a neighbor's dog, the parent must feel comfortable with the children going into the neighbor's home, be sure the dog is friendly, and scout out a safe walking route for the children. So, when marketing this business, do so only within a trusted community, such as your neighborhood, church, and/or school. Make sure you accompany your children if you don't know and trust the person they are working for.

  Once you've ruled out any safety concerns, identify who could use this service. Can you put it on the bulletin board in your local coffee house? What about at your children's school or church or the parent's workplace? Parent Facebook groups provide a great place to offer up your children's services as well.

- *Create marketing materials.* Business cards, although seemingly only for the uber-professional, are super inexpensive and easy to create through sites like Vistaprint. Or you can create them for free through Microsoft Word. Plus, they will make your children feel important.

  Create a business card with their name, your e-mail, and service provided. Do the same for a flyer, and make sure you have this file ready electronically so you can e-mail it out as well. This is where you can have fun with your children and get creative. Create a business name, design a logo, and work with different colors and designs.

- *Set the rules.* Discuss priorities with your children, and make sure this will not interfere with any other commitments, such as school, friends, and after-school activities. Establish when they can work, how many hours per week, and how many hours total they need to reach their savings goal. Talk about any other additional safety issues.

BOOKS FOR LEARNING

- *Arthur's Funny Money* by Lillian Hoban. A funny kids' story about the beloved Arthur character that weaves in business and financial concepts throughout the tale.

- *Amelia Bedelia Means Business* by Herman Parish. The *New York Times* best seller follows Amelia Bedelia as she does whatever it takes to buy a new bike.

ONLINE RESOURCES

- *How to Make Money as a Kid.* This website provides advice and ideas on just that, how to make money as a kid. It provides over 200 business ideas for kids.
  https://www.howtomakemoneyasakid.com/ways-to-make-money-as-a-kid/
- *Allowance & Chores Bot.* Want to go digital with allowance? This $2.99 app keeps track of your children's weekly allowance activities and how much allowance they receive.
  http://wingboat.com/Allowance-Chores-Bot.html

SHORT AND SWEET TAKEAWAYS

1. Allowance is one of the best opportunities to teach children about money. You can decide to tie allowance to chores or not or create a hybrid system. What's important is you do what works for your family, are consistent and positive, and set the expectations.
2. Regardless of your children's age, they can "get a job"! At this point, their job should be something easy and fun and let them earn a little extra money. The goal of a job at a young age is simply to teach them valuable lessons about money and working.

NOTE

1. RoosterMoney. 2018. "The Allowance Report." Accessed September 3, 2018. https://www.roostermoney.com/pocket-money-resources/allowance-report-us

8

Responsible Spending

Responsible spending is like dieting—we all know what we *should* do, but few of us actually do it. It's hard for most people, and you may worry that if *you* don't spend responsibly, how could you possibly teach your children to spend responsibly? Don't worry, even if you have a difficult time curbing your own spending, you can still help your children learn the right ways to spend money. By teaching them these important skills early, they can make mistakes without any consequences. So don't worry if it's not perfect; they have plenty of time to practice before their mistakes actually matter!

Chapter 6 taught your children how to prioritize what they spend money on and differentiate needs from wants. They learned what skills they need to develop in order to make smart spending decisions. This chapter will build on this and apply these skills. It will teach children at an early age the importance of budgeting and smart shopping in simple and realistic ways. The goal in this chapter is not to tell them what to spend their money on, but rather give them the tools to make smart decisions as they get older.

You have an advantage in your corner when teaching responsible spending; opportunities to teach are all around us every day! The skills they need, such as decision-making and prioritizing, are ones they are already learning to develop. They just need to be fine-tuned through practice, like when you go shopping, and through everyday conversations.

START WITH CASH

As with most of the lessons in this book, it's important to be realistic with how money is actually used today. Very few adults whip out $163.28 at the grocery store; most use their debit or credit card. Payment processor TSYS conducted a study in 2017 that asked over 1,000 consumers which payment form they prefer: 44% chose debit cards, 33% selected credit cards, and only 12% specified a preference for using cash.[1]

While certainly the trend is moving toward less cash and more credit and debit cards, we are not yet a cashless society. Because children have a better time understanding something they can see and interact with, this spending chapter teaches the basics with cash. Once the foundation is set, your children can start to explore cashless options, such as debit and credit cards. How to introduce your children to some of these payment methods will be addressed at the end of the chapter. Person-to-person (P2P) payments and electronic wallets are becoming more popular, but most likely won't be relevant to your children until they are older.

SAVE, SPEND, AND SHARE PIGGY BANKS

Since the spend chapter is the first of the three *Piggy Banks* introduced, this is when you'll introduce the three piggy bank system to your children. Begin by getting three clear containers. Although decorative piggy banks may be cute, it's helpful if the containers are clear so your children can actually *see* their money grow. There are hundreds to choose from, and many have fancy features, such as digital coin counting. Although fun, this level of sophistication (and cost!) is not necessary. A simple mason jar with a coin slot lid works beautifully.

Once you have the jars, label them with SAVE, SPEND, and SHARE. Explain to your children that each time they get money, whether through allowance or gifts, they will split their money between three jars. You have already worked through Chapter 7, which introduces allowance, so they now have real money to put in their jars. (This is important, as empty jars are not very motivating!)

The Spend Jar is the easiest to explain. The money in this jar can be spent on everyday items that your children want (with parent approval, of course). This can include small toys when accompanying parents at Target, bouncy balls from a quarter machine at the movies, or an extra arcade game. The point being, this is their money to spend on whatever they want. It's the "Mom/Dad, can I have this?" fund.

The Save Jar is covered in Chapter 9. This is money that your children put away until they need it later. They may be waiting until they have enough money in their Save Jar to buy a new scooter. Or the Save Jar can also be used as a "just in case" fund. This means they will have money just in case they need it, like if they need to fix their bike or there's a new toy they want later.

The Share Jar is discussed in Chapter 10. This is the money that they will use to help others. They can choose to donate it to a charity, buy a gift for disadvantaged children during the holidays, or buy cookies for an elderly neighbor. The purpose of this jar is to help someone who is less fortunate. Chapter 10 will discuss the importance of charity and the many ways young children can get involved.

NEVER TOO YOUNG TO BUDGET

This is the term that most people dread when thinking about finance. You may be thinking that you don't even have your own budget, how in the world will you teach your children about budgeting? Don't worry, this section is not meant to cause anxiety. The purpose of teaching your young children about budgets is not so they will whip out their spreadsheet with every bubble gum purchase. Like most concepts at this age, children need to understand the basics and why budgeting is important. Then, when they are older and making their own money, they will be comfortable managing their own budget.

For those parents who put their hands over their ears and sing "Lala-lalalala!" every time they hear the word budget, here's a reminder of the definition of *budget*: "A record of expenditures and income for a set period of time." Painless enough, right? And most likely, even if you don't officially have a budget, you are "budgeting" every day when you pay your bills, buy groceries, and decide if you can afford a vacation this year.

Practice Activity: Create a Budget

Tell your children that you are going to help them start a budget, which will keep track of how much money they have and spend. Below are easy steps to help them create their budget, using the worksheet found in Figure 8.1.

This won't be exact because your children don't have set expenditures like adults do. Make it loose and hypothetical—it actually makes no difference if the numbers are correct. The purpose is to show them how a budget works. You can completely make up the numbers if you want—just keep it relevant to their spending. You can then update the numbers as your children actually spend their money. This will get them into the habit of thinking about how much money they have and if they have

Monthly Budget		
Money I Will Earn (Income)		
Allowance		$28
Extra Work		$10
Gifts		$0
Other		$0
Total Income		**$38**
Money I Will Spend (Expenses)		
Shopkins Blind Bag		$3
LEGO Harry Potter Aragog's Lair		$15
Play the Virtual Reality game at mall		$10
Total Expenses		**$28**
Money I Will Have Left (Surplus / Deficit)		**$10**

Figure 8.1.   Kid-Friendly Monthly Budget Statement. *Liz Frazier.*

enough for the things they want to buy. Try to review every week when you give your children allowance and make any adjustments.

- *Step 1.* Help your children estimate how much money they will get this month through allowance, extra work, and gifts. List under "Money I Will Earn." Add these up and list total under "Total Income."
- *Step 2.* Ask your children what they want to buy this month. List these items under "Money I Will Spend." Add up all the items, and list total under "Total Expenses."
- *Step 3.* Subtract the amount from Step 2 from the amount in Step 1, and enter under "Money I Will Have Left."

Discussion

Walk them through the numbers at the end. If they end up with a negative amount of money left, it means they spent too much. Look at what they plan to spend money on and see what can be reduced.

Real-World Activity: Prepaid Cards

Time to put that budget into action! Next time you are on a trip with your children (or a concert, amusement park, or any special occasion where you would probably buy them a memento), help them budget by purchasing a prepaid card for them. Although many banks provide prepaid cards, companies are getting into the game now too. FamZoo

(famzoo.com) is a great example; it's geared toward kids and provides valuable money management tools as well.

If taking a trip to Disney World, for example, give them a card with $25 on it (or however much you were planning to spend). Explain to them they will need to plan how they want to spend it because this is all the money they have. This is a great opportunity to use the budget discussed above, to help them think through their purchases. This activity also helps Mom and Dad stay on track with how much money they spend on their kids!

PULL BACK YOUR OWN SPENDING CURTAINS

Once they have an idea of how a budget works, show them yours. Don't panic. Even if you don't have an official budget, you can create one pretty quickly using the worksheet provided in Chapter 2 (Figure 2.2). For the purposes of teaching your children, you can just estimate. Show your children what your *need* items are each month and how much money is left after you buy them. Then, show them how you can spend only whatever money is left on your *want* items. Engage in the same discussion as you did after they created their own budget. Where do you spend too much? What are some changes you could make?

It's really important to keep this activity positive—you don't want to stress your children out or make them worry about the family's financial health. If you don't have a budget and realize only after creating your quickie version that you are way in the red . . . fudge the numbers a bit to show your children a "happier" version. However, if you are reviewing a budget that stresses you out about your own finances too much, skip this activity. Your children will feel your anxiety, and they will equate budgets and finances with stress. (Then, be sure to review and evaluate your budget later, when your children are not around, to see where you could make changes to get on the right track.)

Practice Activity: Allocating Dollars

First, calculate what percentage you spend of your monthly income on your fixed bills. For example, if you bring home $3,000/month and your power costs $100 each month, 3.3% goes to power. If rent is $1,000 each month, approximately 30% of your income goes to rent. Repeat this for each of your major expenses.

Next, take out $100 (or whatever amount works for your budget) in $1 bills. Your children will already be mesmerized by this. Tell them, for the purpose of this activity, this is how much money you make each month.

Next, allocate your money into piles for each bill. For example, you would take 3% of the $100 (three $1 dollar bills) and put it into the "power bill pile." Then thirty $1 bills will go into the "rent pile." Do this for each of your bills. The goal is to show your children how much money goes to your needs and what you have left over for your wants. Your children (and you!) will be amazed by how much money you had in the beginning and how quickly it all disappeared. It's also an interesting way to see what is considered the most valuable and why.

Pretend Play: Living on Your Own

This is a fun game for all ages, and you can play with multiple people. Have your children pretend like they've moved out of the house and are living on their own. Their new "home" can be a tent, their room, or a fort outside. Give them $100 pretend money and tell them it's for one month of living. The object is to illustrate budgeting and needs versus wants in the real world. The children win the round if they pay all of their fixed expenses and stay under budget.

- *The budget.* In this activity, they are graduating to a more realistic budget that separates expenses into fixed and discretionary—or more appropriately, "needs" and "wants." Figure 8.2 includes an example of a budget that can be used for this game. The total amounts are blank; fill them in and balance the budget with your children after each round.
- *Setup.* Set up stations corresponding with the need and want expenses listed on the budget. Make it as elaborate as you want. Stock up the grocery store with food from the kitchen. You can fill the vet clinic with doctor tools and stuffed animals, or there can simply be a piece of paper with the word "Vet" on it. The point is that each need and want expense should have its own station.
- *Roles.* This is best played with several people so each person can have a different role. One owns the grocery store, one is the landlord, one is the fun amusement park worker, and so on. If it's just you and your child . . . well, get your sneakers on and be ready for an active morning.
- *Rules.*
  - Explain to them that they are now an adult and get to make their own decisions. They have their own money and can spend it how they want. The hope is that they now understand the importance of prioritizing and putting needs before wants . . . but you may have to give them a few nudges in the right direction.
  - Once the game starts, you are no longer Mom and Dad. You are an uncaring landlord, a dazzling amusement park owner, or a

stressed grocery store owner. Stay strong. Don't give them any tips or warnings . . . remember that they are now an adult!

- One month is 10 minutes (or whatever works for your children—just set it in advance with a timer). Plan for multiple months so you can switch roles around.
- If at the end of each "month," they don't pay all of their "need" amounts, they lose. For every day that they spend responsibly and pay all of their bills, they get a reward or treat.
- Have fun and get into character! If they lose because they forgot to pay the power bill, turn off all the lights and make it pitch black. Make the movie theater and amusement park really fun, and try to distract your children from paying their bills. After all, this is meant to be like real life!

Discussion

Go through the days they won and talk about what they did well and how they prioritized and made good decisions. On the days they lost, help your children pinpoint what they could have done differently.

Monthly Budget	
Money I Will Earn	
Salary	$100
Total Income	**$100**
Needs (Fixed Expenses)	
Rent for House	$30
Power	$10
Food	$20
Vet for Dog	$10
Total Fixed Expenses	*$$$*
Wants (Discretionary Expenses)	
Each Toy	$10
Amusement Park Ride	$10
Movie	$10
Arcade Game	$10
Total Discretionary Expenses	*$$$*
Total Expenses (Needs + Wants)	**$$$**
Surplus / Deficit (Income – Total Expenses)	**$$$**

Figure 8.2. Game Budget. *Liz Frazier.*

Real-World Activity: School Accounts

Many kids in elementary schools now have some form of electronic money account with their school, usually used for drinks, snacks, and lunches. Parents can add money into their children's account, and the children can use as they need. If your school has this system, let your children practice budgeting with their accounts.

Start small by telling them that this week you will put $5 (or whatever is appropriate for your children) on their card and they can spend it however they want. The key is to tell them that they will not get any more money that week so they need to decide how to spend their money smartly. If they load up on snacks Monday morning and run out of money, they may have to bring their snacks from home the rest of the week.

Obviously, it's not recommended to let your children starve at lunch because they didn't budget properly, so this works best if the school money is initially meant for only extra snacks for your children, not their lunch. Then, you can up the stakes as they get older. Give them money for the full month. You can then try including lunch in their budget. If they use their money before the end of the month, they will have to make their own lunch at home to bring to school.

Your children will learn firsthand what a budget is and why it's important. And the best part? If they make a mistake, they will feel real consequences and not want to make that same mistake again.

SMART SHOPPING

Whether you are shopping for them or running errands, use your daily activities as opportunities to teach your children five core smart shopping strategies:

1. *Avoid impulse buying.*

   - *Make a list.* Making a list before going to the grocery store helps reduce impulse decisions. Have your children help you list everything you need before leaving the house. Once you are at the store, give them a few items to find on their own. Then, when they ask if they can have something else, remind them that it's not on the list.
   - *Wait.* If your children want something that is expensive, make them wait 24 hours before purchasing. Tell them if they are still interested in the item after a day, you will take them back to get it. If they forget about it, it clearly wasn't that important. Set a dollar limit for what's considered expensive based on their age and allowance, like $10 for a kindergartener and $20 for a fourth-grader.

- *Set a limit at events.* One-time events, like shows, circuses, carnivals, and amusement parks, get everyone excited, especially children. You will barely have stepped inside before hearing all the things they want (must we relive the Minion doll!). Before going to an event, give your children a limit on how much they can spend. This will cut down on the wands, fans, bubble makers, Styrofoam fingers, and other cheap items they will buy and instantly break.

2. *Focus on saving money.*

    - *Bring coupons.* Even if you're not a regular coupon cutter, doing it with your children provides the valuable lesson of saving money while shopping. Have your children help you find the coupon items while at the store. Show them how much money you saved at the end of the trip.
    - *Comparison shop.* Whether it's food or something for yourself, make a point of comparison shopping. Look at several similar items and how much each one costs. Explain to your children that you want to find the least expensive choice but it still needs to be good quality. Show them the price differences between brand name items and generic; encourage them to buy generic when the quality is the same. Identify any specials going on at the store, and explain how products sometimes go on sale when a store wants to sell more of that product.
    - *Buy in bulk.* When you can, buy items in bulk, and show your children how you can save money doing this by comparing the individual costs of an item.

3. *Think before you buy.*

    - *Research.* If there is an item your children want, explain that there are several different types of that item so it's important to buy the right one. For example, if your children want a float for the pool, help them research different types of floats. Read reviews and compare the qualities of several models. Include them when you are researching items that you plan to purchase for yourself. Ask them which one is better quality and which they think you should buy.
    - *Other options.* If your children really want something, look at options other than buying it. Is this something you can rent or borrow from the library or a friend? Can you buy it used and save some money?

4. *Stop buying "stuff."*

    - This is so much easier said than done, especially when your first-grader is standing in the aisle screaming that he will "die" if he doesn't get that high-flying bouncy ball. Stand strong. Unless you are going shopping with the intent to buy him something, stop buying him those little knick-knacks whose sole purpose of existence is to keep him happy (and quiet) so you can shop in peace. Make him bring his own money and tell him that he can use that to buy the bouncy ball.

5. *Rewards.*

   • While this may go against everything listed here, you don't want to make shopping and spending money a torturous activity for your children. Make sure you *occasionally* splurge a little with them. (The key word here is *occasionally*.)

SETTING A POSITIVE EXAMPLE

You can set an example every day by following some of the tips below. Be sure to explain to your children what you're doing and how it saves money.

• *Save on power.* So much money is spent each day on power. Make it a point to turn off the lights when you leave the room, and ask your children to do the same. When you leave the house, ask your children to go through each room and make sure the lights are turned off. This has the added bonus of saving you money each month!
• *Movie nights.* What used to be a cheap night out now costs almost the same as a weekend getaway. A family of four going out for dinner and a movie can cost upward of $200, especially if you add in the necessary staples, like the 45-ounce soda and jumbo popcorn. This is not to say that your family should *never* go to the movies. Just occasionally tell your children that you are going to try to save some money and, instead of going out to the movies tonight, you're going to have "movie night" at home. Pop some popcorn, turn down the lights, and rent a movie or watch one you've previously purchased.
• *Carpool.* Gas prices are always on the rise and oftentimes not calculated in one's everyday expenses or factored in when planning an outing. Carpool with other parents the next time you have to travel for your child's soccer game. Tell your child that you saved money by splitting the cost of gas.
• *Handmade gifts.* Instead of buying all of your gifts this year, try making a few. Encourage your children to make their own gifts, such as jewelry, poems, drawings, or cookies for their friends and family at birthdays and holidays. Not only is this a great way to save some money; it's also thoughtful and can be fun.

BOOKS FOR LEARNING

- *Alexander Who Used to Be Rich Last Sunday* by Judith Viorst. This book tells yet another tale of the misadventures of the adored and misunderstood Alexander. In this book, he gets a dollar from his grandparents and is faced with all the ways he could spend it. This book provides valuable lessons and is an entertaining look at how *not* to spend money.

ONLINE RESOURCES

- *Moneyandstuff.info* provides financial games and activities for kids, specifically focusing on tools to help kids create budgets. http://moneyandstuff.info/budget-worksheets/
- *Mint.com*, in addition to many other financial resources, provides a fun quiz to determine your children's spending personality http://www.themint.org/kids/what-kind-of-spender-are-you.html.
- *RoosterMoney* is a digital tool that lets kids keep track of their allowance while allowing parents to oversee their spending. https://www.roostermoney.com/us

SHORT AND SWEET TAKEAWAYS

1. Get started on the Spend, Save, and Share Piggy Bank system—have your children split everything they earn into these three jars!
2. It is never too early to learn how to budget. Teach your kids the basics by using examples of what they earn and spend; also, share examples from your budget.
3. You are your children's primary teacher! Be sure you are leading by example and teaching your children good habits.

NOTE

1. TSYS. 2017. "2017 Consumer Payment Study." Accessed September 3, 2018. https://www.tsys.com/Assets/TSYS/downloads/rs_2017-us-consumer-payment-study.pdf.

9

🌡️

Saving

We all know the *real* reason every parent is reading this book. You are hoping that after reading this book with your seven-year-old child, she will turn to you and say, "You know what, Mom? I really think it's time that I start saving for college." Unfortunately, at this age that's about as realistic as your children telling you that they plan to cut down on sugar this year.

That being said, this chapter will teach you how to lay the foundation now with your children by starting small and getting them excited about saving. It will show you how to build upon that foundation, which then leads to developing smart financial habits that will last your children a lifetime. Why is this so important? If they save when they are young, they are more likely to save when they are older. A strong savings account as an adult means protection, peace of mind, and opportunities.

Like the other chapters, this chapter starts off using "real" coins and bills so the kids can touch, feel, and play with actual money. Once they are comfortable (or a bit older), Chapter 12 moves to opening a bank account, using digital tools, and learning more complex concepts.

WHY TEACH YOUNG CHILDREN ABOUT SAVING?

If you decide to teach your children only one thing from this book, it should be how to save. Learning to save at a young age teaches important skills, such as setting goals, patience, and determination. Saving also has tangible results as an adult: avoiding debt, obtaining financial security, and meeting long-term goals, like buying a house and preparing for re-tirement. These are needs that most adults struggle with today.

According to the Government Accountability Office (GAO), around 29% of households that include individuals aged 55 and older have nei-ther retirement savings nor a pension. Around half of American house-holds have no retirement accounts at all.[1] Teaching children the funda-mentals of saving gives them a chance for a more secure future.

Although it would be nice, at age six we're not expecting our children to start saving for retirement. As discussed, they probably won't make a dent in college savings either right now. Most likely at this age their saving goals will be small and short term. They will save up their money for something specific and then spend it all. And that is perfectly fine because they are just learning and becoming comfortable with the concept of saving.

The beauty of learning at this age is consequences don't matter. If they can't save enough money for an American Girl doll, the only consequence is they just won't get the doll. Soon enough, the consequences of saving or not saving will become very real. When they are out of college and mak-ing real money, it matters a great deal if they can save. Learning how to "pay themselves first" by putting away a percentage of every allowance will help them get in the habit of saving in the future. Take a look at Text-box 9.1 for an example of the power of starting to save early.

TEXTBOX 9.1. SAVING EXAMPLE

The Tale of Bella and Henry

Bella: Bella's parents taught her to save from a young age. At 22, when she graduated college, she got an assistant job at a PR firm making $45,000/year. As she always did with her allowance, she continues to put away 20% of each paycheck—about $600/month.

Henry: Bella is still in touch with her childhood friend, Henry. Henry's parents were never comfortable talking about finances and therefore never discussed the importance of savings with Henry. Henry got the same job as Bella, worked in the cube next to her, and made the same salary. However, Henry didn't think about putting away any of his money until, at the age of 32, he attended an HR presentation that suggested saving in his 401(k).

At age 62, Henry and Bella meet to catch up over lunch. Awkwardly and conveniently, the conversation turned to how much money they had saved. Henry saved $600/month for 30 years, with 8% interest and was proud of the $851,168 he has accumulated. Bella has been saving the same dollar amount as Henry but started 10 years earlier. She has amassed a whopping $1,945,682 and is about to retire early!

This is a simplified example. This assumes Bella and Henry don't spend any of their savings, don't increase the amount saved as their income rises, and the interest rate stays constant. The point is, Bella has more than double Henry and started only 10 years earlier. When it comes to saving, the power of time is undeniable. The money Bella saved from age 22 to 32 had 30-plus years to accumulate interest. Like everything else, the habits learned as children, whether positive or negative, will carry through to adulthood; you want your kids to automatically start saving out of habit when it starts to count.

Note: This type of calculation is easy to do with the help of an online calculator, such as the one found on Bankrate: https://www.bankrate .com/calculators/savings/simple-savings-calculator.aspx.

SAVING VERSUS SPENDING

Since your children learned about spending in Chapter 8, an easy way to explain saving is to show them the differences between the two. Get out your children's Spend and Save Jars. Count out all the money in each (if you don't have any yet, just make up a pretend amount). Tell them the major difference between the two is the Spend Jar is for things they want to buy *now*; the Save Jar is for things they want to buy *in the future*. It's for the bigger things that they want to buy but need to wait until they have enough money.

Pop Quiz: Save or Spend Jar?

Give your children examples of different items and ask if they would use the money from their Save or Spend Jar. For the Save Jar items, help them come up with a plan on how they could save for it. Remember, at this stage it's not meant to be perfect or exact. These examples are simple, but they are meant to be simple. The goal is to introduce these concepts to them so they start *thinking about saving* and become comfortable with the concept. A few examples that you can ask your children are below, but you can use anything relevant to your children. Start off by telling them they have $10 in their Spend Jar and $20 in their Save Jar. (The answers are at the end of the book on page 146.)

1. You are at the grocery store and see the cutest stuffed animal unicorn. You have to have it, and the price is $4. Does this come out of your Spend Jar or Save Jar?

2. You are with your parents at the arcade and want to play one more game, but your parents say you have to use your own money. Each game costs $2. Does this come out of your Save Jar or Spend Jar?

3. a. You are at your friend's house who has the most amazing remote-controlled airplane. You tell your dad you want the same one; together you look up the price, which is $40. Which jar will this come out of? (Help your children think through this question until you determine that they don't have enough money in their Spend Jar so this is something they will need to save for.)

   b. The second part of this question is to then come up with a plan. They have $20 in their Save Jar. They get $9/week in allowance and put $3 in the Save Jar each week. How long will it take until they have saved up enough money?

   c. If that seems like a long time to them, walk through ways they could save more, such as doing odd jobs around the house to earn extra money or putting more money in the Save Jar and less in the Spend Jar. Or they could allocate money meant for the Spend Jar toward the airplane.

YOU ARE ALREADY TEACHING YOUR CHILDREN TO SAVE

It's called *delayed gratification*. You are already teaching your children that they have to wait for the things they want now. Parents teach their children this all the time while waiting for the swings or standing in line for ice cream. By teaching your children to wait patiently, you are giving them a foundation to learn how to save.

A famous example of delayed gratification is a series of studies conducted at Stanford University called the *Marshmallow Test*.[2] In these studies, children were offered a choice between one marshmallow provided immediately or two marshmallows if they waited for a short period. The tester would then leave the children alone in the room with the marshmallow. They would return about 15 minutes later to see who ate the treat and who had the willpower to resist (delayed gratification).

In follow-up studies over the next 40 years, the researchers found that the children who were able to wait for the two marshmallows tended to have better life outcomes, as measured by SAT scores, educational attainment, health, and other life measures.

Real-World Activity: Marshmallow Test

You can conduct your own Marshmallow Test with your children. Next time you are at the store, give your children $5. Tell them they have two options: (1) they can buy whatever they want for $5 now, or (2) if they don't spend it today, they can have an additional $5 to spend at the store tomorrow, for a total of $10 (use whatever dollar amounts will work for them). Or if not a specific dollar amount, you can use specific toy examples ("You can have either the small LEGO set now, or if you wait until the end of the week, you can get the bigger one").

If you use the $5 example, they will initially look around to see what they can get now. Help them shop around and show them examples of what they could get for $10 if they "save" their money and wait. You will see their wheels turning as they shop and determine that it may be better to wait. Ultimately, let them make their own decision.

Discussion

Follow up with your children the next day about the decision they made. If they chose to buy something instead of waiting, ask them if they are happy with their decision. Or better yet, ask if they are still enjoying their purchase (odds are, like most young kids, they have forgotten all about that $5 toy they bought yesterday).

TEACHING BY EXAMPLE

One of the most important ways to teach your children to save is by example. Talk to your children about what you are saving for and why.

- Some examples are easy, such as saving for a new house or a big trip. Tell them why it's important to you, what your savings goal is, and how you plan to reach it.
- When you're at the store, make a point of telling them when there's something you want but you are not going to get it because you are saving for something else. Again, you are teaching them delayed gratification and also *opportunity costs*, which means the benefit of giving up one thing for another (discussed in Chapter 11).
- For retirement, explain to them that you are saving up enough money so that you don't have to work when you get older.
- To explain the rationale for saving money for an "emergency" or "just in case" fund, use one of their toys as an example. If they have a beloved bike, ask them what would happen if someday the tire popped. They'll respond that they have to get it fixed. Explain to them that they would need money to get it fixed, so people need to have a "just in case" fund to use when something breaks and needs fixing. Emergency fund can sound scary to some little ones.

PUMP THE BRAKES ON BUYING

What is the hardest, but probably the most valuable, lesson you can teach your children about saving? Stop buying them everything they ask for. "Easier said than done," says the parent with the screaming five-year-old at Target. It's hard, and we are all guilty of taking the easy way out and just buying the item for them. It will take a while to break this habit, but start telling the children no when they ask for something not needed. Tell them for things like this, they need to use their Spend Jar or save up for what they want to buy.

The more you say no, the easier it gets because your children will stop expecting you to buy them items just because they ask (or demand). If you follow through and your children really believe that you won't buy them that coveted Harry Potter wand, they will quickly look for ways to buy it themselves.

Real-World Activity: Saving for a Goal

The best way for your children to understand how to save is to engage them; make saving relevant and exciting with the activity below:

- *Create a saving goal.* Ask your children to think about something they really want. Together, come up with one (relatively) big ticket item for your children to save for. However, make sure it's an attainable goal because you don't want them to get discouraged by not being able to reach it. If your children are on the younger side, don't pick a $500 bike for their first experience in saving. The point is to get them excited about saving and understand the concept. Saving goals could be things like a $25 terrarium kit or a $48 VTech Smartwatch.
- *Goal poster.* Once you have identified the item, create a "goal poster." Get a thick piece of construction paper or poster board. On one side, tape or draw a picture of the object. This will serve as motivation for saving (and will help them remember . . . the mind of a young one shifts rapidly!). On the other side, draw (or print out) the goal chart. This can be the classic thermometer, or you can get creative based on what your children like, such as a rocket or a castle. See Figure 9.1 for fun goal chart ideas.
- *Savings plan.* This is when you can introduce a little simple math to your children. Based on how much they get in allowance and the cost of the object, make a plan for how they will reach their savings goal.

   For example, your seven-year-old daughter is saving for the LEGO City Race Car, which at your local toy store costs $48. There are several paths to get to her goal. Let's say she gets an allowance of

$7/week and $3 of that goes to her Save Jar. If she uses only her allowance to save up for the car, she'll be able to afford it in 16 weeks ($48/$3). Sixteen weeks is four months, which might as well be four years to a seven-year-old. If your child is that rare breed of children who can wait that long (she or he obviously would pass the Marshmallow Test with flying colors), then you can make a straightforward savings plan over 16 weeks. However, if your children need help getting to their goal faster, here are a few options:

- Offer a matching program. For example, this could be a dollar for dollar match until they reach their goal. With $3 saved each week and $3 matched, your children would really need to raise only $24 total, which would take eight weeks. Or you can match their money when they reach the halfway point. Structure it based on what works for your family.
- Offer additional ways to earn money through extra chores. This has the dual benefit of teaching your children to work for their money and provides you with some needed help around the house.

- *Create milestones.* Once you've come up with your savings plan, add in several milestones with rewards on your goal chart. The milestones can be percentages of the total goal or specific dollar amounts. The rewards can be anything that would incentivize them, like an ice cream sundae, movie night, or matched money for their savings. The idea here is to customize it to your children and make it fun and engaging. Get creative!
- *Follow through.* While some unique children may be able to stay focused and motivated on something for a full month (or even longer!), most will need some help. It's up to you to help them follow through on their savings goal. Find a time, maybe after dinner at the end of the week or at allowance time, to look at the chart and discuss where they are and how much they need.

  Make a big deal out of it every time they add to their Save Jar. Use a marker to fill up the goal chart as they save to show them their progress. Don't worry if halfway through your children decide they want the Silly Scents Sticker Maker instead of the race car. Just change the chart as needed and roll with it. The purpose of this exercise is to teach your children how to save—it doesn't matter what they save for at this point.
- *Do it together.* A great way to engage your children is to save together. Identify something you need to save for also, and together, you can celebrate each other's wins. This also helps continue the discussion around savings goals and makes it a part of your daily conversations.

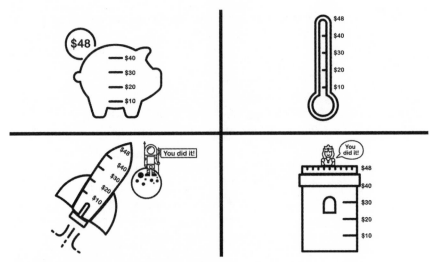

Figure 9.1. Goal Posters. *Kristen Buchholz.*

Discussion

Obviously, you will talk about this as they are saving but be sure to follow up after they have reached their goal. Ask them what was the hardest part about it? Do they feel proud now that they have reached their goal? What's the next thing they want to save for?

BOOKS FOR LEARNING

- *Blueberries for Sal* by Robert McCloskey. This is one of the great classic kids' books, which happens to have valuable savings lessons. The story is about a little girl named Sal who picks blueberries with her mother on a mountain while a bear cub and his mother eat berries on the other side of the same mountain. At the end of the book, ask your children why Sal's mother didn't want her to eat all the blueberries (they were saving them for winter). This can lead to a simple conversation about saving; sometimes, we have to wait, rather than do what we want now (again, delayed gratification!).
- *Little Critter: Just Saving My Money* by Mercer Mayer. Who doesn't remember and love the Little Critter books? A timeless character, Little Critter wants a new skateboard, but his dad makes him work to save for it. Straightforward lessons taught throughout the pages, and all children can relate to the sweet Little Critter.

ONLINE RESOURCES

- *Visa Practical Money Skills* provides savings games for kids.
  http://www.practicalmoneyskills.com/play
- *BizKids* teaches practical money skills for entrepreneurial kids through games, lessons, and shows.
  http://bizkids.com/
- *TheMint.com* has a simple and interactive site dedicated to teaching kids financial literacy.
  http://themint.org/
- *InCharge Debt Solutions* provides financial lessons and activities for parents, teachers, and kids.
  https://www.incharge.org/financial-literacy/resources-for-teachers/financial-literacy-for-kids/
- *Peter Pig* is an app that uses games for kids to practice identifying, counting, and saving money while learning fun facts about US currency.
  http://practicalmoneyskills.com/play/peter_pigs_money_counter
- *WisePockets* uses a "choose your own adventure" style online book to teach kids about saving, spending, and earning.
  http://www.umsl.edu/~wpockets/Clubhouse/library.htm
- *Warren Buffett's Secret Millionaires Club* is an animated series that features Warren Buffett and teaches the basics of good financial decision-making.
  http://smckids.com/about.php

SHORT AND SWEET TAKEAWAYS

1. The goal of this chapter is to teach your children to always, *always* "pay themselves first."
2. The Spend Jar is for items they want to buy now. The Save Jar is for bigger items that they will buy in the future.
3. Teach how to save by example. Talk through day-to-day saving examples with your children as well as bigger examples, like retirement or a new house.

NOTES

1. U.S. Government Accountability Office. 2015. "Most Households Approaching Retirement Have Low Savings." Accessed September 3, 2018. https://www.gao.gov/products/GAO-15-419.

2. Wikipedia. n.d. "Stanford marshmallow experiment." Modified August 2018. https://en.wikipedia.org/wiki/Stanford_marshmallow_experiment.

10

Sharing

All parents want to raise generous children who understand the importance of charity and giving back. However, teaching this to kids can be easier said than done. If you're like many adults, most of your charity comes from your wallet, and financial donations can be a hard concept to teach children. Or you may want your children to be involved, but worry they are too young to participate or understand.

One of the most valuable financial lessons your children can learn at a young age is how to use money for good, but learning this doesn't actually begin with money. While financial support is incredibly important, what comes first at this age is cultivating the natural compassion and generosity within each child. Charity doesn't have to be about giving donations or even volunteering with an official organization. In fact, most parents are already teaching their children about charity and its many forms, whether it's through a kind word, a letter to a nursing home, or offering to help an elderly neighbor with yard work.

You can then apply these same principles to giving financially. And although it may seem that they aren't contributing much financially now, every little bit matters. Every penny given of their hard-earned money makes a positive impact not only on the community but also on the children themselves. And the little they give now will grow as they grow. By instilling these values in them now, giving will continue to be a part of their everyday lives. The children who are taught to give back while young will be able to change the world as adults.

The first section of this chapter explains charity and giving and provides ways to incorporate it in your children's lives. Once they understand the importance of giving back, section two will build on those values with real-world ways to help and share. The Share Jar will be introduced here with the goal of building the habit to give a little back anytime you earn money.

SECTION I: THE FUNDAMENTALS OF SHARING

WHY TEACH YOUNG CHILDREN ABOUT SHARING?

You may feel your children are too young to learn about sharing and giving. Or maybe you want to shield your children from the bad things that happen in the world. However, there are many reasons to start teaching your children about giving back at a young age.

- *Shows them that they can make an impact.* Although your children may not be the heroes that save the whales today, they will be heroes to your elderly neighbors whose lawns they mow. Young children can make a huge difference by committing the smallest acts of kindness.
- *Encourages positive habits.* Anyone with young children understands that, if there is something you want your children to learn when they are older, start them early (go back to the example about teaching a 14-year-old to swim; that's a fun summer). If they start early, they will naturally incorporate these lessons into their day-to-day lives as they get older. Charity will then become a priority as they mature.
- *Reminds your children to be kind.* Again, we all want kind children. If everyone were kind, this world would be a better place.
- *Builds self-esteem.* Kids love to be helpful. When children help others, it provides a sense of accomplishment that makes them feel useful, proud, and worthy.
- *Creates the butterfly effect.* In the natural world, the butterfly effect is how the smallest change in one thing can result in large differences in a later state. The name comes from the idea that a butterfly flapping its wings could eventually have a far-reaching ripple effect on subsequent historic events. Although not proven in terms of human behavior, doesn't it make sense that a small act of kindness by one, positively influences another, who then may be encouraged to help someone else? Why not? This is also referred to as *pay it forward*. Or just plain old good karma.

EXPLAINING CHARITY

Starting the conversation about charity with young children is tough. While you want them to understand how there are many people who need help, they are still children. Don't overwhelm them with the horrors of the world. Start small by discussing what compassion and empathy mean. They will catch on quickly because children at their core are kind. Just look at a playground when another child gets hurt or when a baby sibling cries. Kids instinctually soothe and comfort others. If this trait is nurtured, being charitable will come naturally to them.

Use everyday examples that they can understand, like a friend being sad or how an elderly neighbor may need help. Explain that *charity* means helping someone who is in need and is also called *giving back*. Point out all the ways they are charitable already by performing little acts of kindness, such as trying to cheer up their friend or helping their neighbor up their stairs. When they help their younger sister with a problem, point out how kind and helpful that was. If they come home from school and say that they offered to help the teacher clean her whiteboard, mention how generous that was.

An additional way to explain the importance of charity is to make it personal. Share a story of a time that someone helped you or your family. Your children will learn the concept quickly once they can relate it to their own life or to someone they love. Once this becomes a regular discussion, begin bringing up larger concepts about charity. Again, the goal is not to scare or sadden them, but to show them that there are people in need around the world and there are ways others can help them.

SHOW YOUR CHILDREN THE GOOD

Sadly, the reason charity is so important is because there are so many in need. This is the most apparent when tragedy strikes, whether through a hurricane, earthquake, or attack. When something terrible like this happens, use it as an opportunity to show your children the good in people.

Show them the community drives set up to help those that were hurt. Read them the stories in the news about the people who go straight to the site to help rebuild homes. Your children can become involved simply by donating canned food to a local community drive. Ask your children to think of other ways that they could help. Children are incredibly thoughtful and may think of something that you didn't, such as writing letters of encouragement to the children affected by a tragedy.

START AT HOME

Getting your children actively involved doesn't mean you need to immediately drop them off at a Habitat for Humanity site for an eight-hour shift. You've already pointed out ways that they are currently charitable through their everyday small acts of kindness. Now that they are aware of the importance of this behavior, strike while the iron is hot! Encourage giving back in new and unique ways, starting with your family.

If Dad is in bed with a cold, suggest to your children that they make him a special breakfast in bed. If Mom is stressed and busy, suggest they wash her car together as a surprise. When younger siblings are sad, encourage your children to think of ways to cheer them up. You are probably already encouraging this kindness every day; this is simply putting it into context for your children.

SET THE EXAMPLE

Although your children may be too young for some activities, you are not! Find a way to involve your children in your charitable or volunteer activities. Below are examples:

- *Take them with you to donate blood.* If this is something that terrifies you, don't feel you have to be a hero in front of your children. What better way to teach the true meaning of charity than by doing something you're scared of? Also, children love to be the strong ones, so give them the chance to comfort you for a change. *Parent tip:* They won't be able to sit right next to you for safety reasons, so have them bring a book, homework, or drawing materials to keep busy.
- *Be generous in your everyday life.* Welcome others into your home. Bring your children with you to deliver food to a friend after she's had a baby. Be generous with your friendship and time.
- *Make it a family activity.* Whatever the activity, try to include the whole family. It's so impactful for your children to see that giving is important to the family as a unit. Plus, doing good together brings the family closer together.
- *Share throughout the year, not just holidays.* The holidays are such clear opportunities to give, but don't forget that those same people need help every month of the year.
- *Volunteer your time for your children's activities.* Volunteer with their school, church, or community center. They will feel the effects firsthand of how someone's generosity can make an impact. Plus, it sets the example for them. This also shows them the importance of being

part of something bigger than themselves and how much a group of people can accomplish.

• *Let them help with preparations.* If they are too young to help you at the soup kitchen, maybe they can help you prepare the food at home to bring. If you are throwing a fundraiser, let them help you decorate.

ENCOURAGE GRATITUDE

In addition to being kind and compassionate, another everyday behavior to nurture is gratitude. Explain to your children that there are some people who have more and some people who have less than they have. If they have food to eat, a warm home, and a loving family, they are some of the lucky ones.

The best way to do this is through example. Show your appreciation for the little things in life, and your children will be less likely to take things for granted. Ask your children what they are thankful for or to list three good things that happened today. A general sense of gratitude encourages compassion and fuels the desire to give back.

SECTION II: GET INVOLVED

LITTLE THINGS MATTER

This is a good time to slow down and start to help your children identify ways to give back in everyday situations. When you're with your children in line for coffee, try paying for a coffee for the person in line behind you. Your children will have a million questions ("Why did you do that? Do you know them? What if they don't want coffee?"). You can explain to them that you have the money and thought that surprising someone with coffee would be a nice thing to do.

Ask them how they would feel if they had a bad day at school and at the end of the day found a bag of Skittles taped to their cubby. It would not only cheer up their mood (because who doesn't love Skittles?), but it would also make them feel happy that someone cares about them. Ask them what types of things they could do for others to surprise them.

Same goes for things like leaving a note on a stranger's car that says, "Have a nice day!" This is not something that most people do on a daily basis, but it's a great way to show your children that they can do simple things that can make one person a little happier.

Real-World Activity: The Giving Project

Have your children start their own charitable project. Tell them it can be anything they want, as long as it helps someone or is in some way doing good.

- *Brainstorm.* To start, work with your children to identify a cause. To make the most meaningful impact on your children, they should be actively involved and able to relate to the cause. Talk with your children about their passions and interests to see how you can match those up with a charitable project.

    If they love art, they could make cards for the local nursing home. Do you have a social butterfly? Throw a donation party where the kids bring a gently used toy to donate to a local homeless shelter. If your children are obsessed with dogs, what better way to show it than volunteering at an animal shelter? Kids get excited about coming up with ways they can help others; let their imaginations run wild.
- *Sort out the details.* Do they need money for this project? Do they need a group of people to do it? How much time will it take?
- *Get your children excited about it.* This should be a hands-on experience, so let them make decisions on how to execute it. The more involved they are, the more meaningful it is to them.
- *Most importantly, have patience.* Although your children are naturally kind and compassionate, they are just learning how to apply it in a structured setting. Volunteer and charity work should always be viewed in a positive way by your children, never as a punishment or something that's forced on them. Think of it like potty training—only use praise and positive support so they actually want to continue doing it.

Discussion

Before the activity, talk to your children about what it means and how they are helping. Be sure to recap with your children afterward. Did they enjoy it? How do they think they helped? What else could they do? What were some things they could have done better? What are they most proud of?

CHARITABLE ACTIVITIES FOR KIDS

There are countless ways every day that children can get involved. Below are examples of unstructured activities that children of any age can do at any time. Note that parents should always supervise young children, no matter what the activity.

- *Hand out drinks.* On cold days, hand out coffee or cocoa to neighborhood workers, mailmen, or garbage truck drivers. Hand out lemonade or water on hot days.
- *Pick up litter.* Pick up litter at school or church or around your neighborhood or park. (Remember to wear gloves!)
- *Make a family charity activity.* Participate in a walk for charity together or have your children help you cook something for an elderly family member.
- *Donate toys and clothes.* Set your children up carefully for this because it can quickly turn into a tearful disaster ("But I *love* this toy [that I haven't played with all year]!"). There are several ways you can broach the subject. One, try being direct: "Wow, you have so many toys. I see a few that you haven't played with in a long time. You know, there are a lot of children who don't have any toys. Would you like to pick out a few toys to give to other children?" This probably has a 50/50 chance of working. If your children give a firm and clear no, don't push it. Come back on a different day with a new tactic.

  Try again at birthday time or on any occasion where they will receive new toys. Tell them that, to have enough room for their new toys, they have to give away some of their old ones. Most kids are so excited at the thought of a new toy, they are eager to replace one of their older toys. However you start the conversation, let them choose the toys and don't expect *too* much. Kids don't see the same value in spring cleaning as adults do.
- *Create cards.* Have your children create cards for a local nursing home or active military.
- *Bake cookies.* Bake cookies with your children to bring over to a new neighbor's house.
- *Deliver treats.* Bring your children with you to deliver treats to local policemen, firefighters, and other service people.
- *Share toys.* Do your children have an enormous train collection or dinosaur set they don't play with often but are not ready to give away? Ask your local library if they would like your children to bring it on occasion to share with the other kids. *Parent tip:* Discuss with your children that some parts may get lost, and make sure they are OK with that. Don't have them bring in their most prized collections.
- *Ask for gifts for charity.* Ask for gifts to charity instead of birthday gifts. This is another tough one for young kids to swallow (understandably). A less extreme option is to ask friends to bring a gently used book or toy to donate in addition to a small gift for your children.

- *Visit pet shelters.* Ask your local pet shelter if you can bring food or toys to the animals.
- *Help out around your neighborhood.* Clean up after a storm or offer to help shovel snow from an elderly neighbor's driveway or rake their leaves.
- *Support volunteers.* If there is a volunteer opportunity your children are too young to participate in, they can support the volunteers by handing out treats to them.

    Parent tip: Make sure you are prepared to either let your children have one of the snacks or bring your own to give them. If younger children are handing out snacks to others but can't have one for themselves, the "handing out" could quickly look a lot more like "throwing snacks in a fit of rage."
- *Throw a "giving party."* There are endless ways to throw a party for a good cause. Throw a craft party where the kids make decorations for a hospital. Or ask the children to bring canned food to donate.
- *Volunteer for Habitat for Humanity.* While the age limit is 16 to actually work on-site, the website provides several options for younger kids to get involved through games, activities, and lessons. https://www.habitat.org/volunteer/near-you/youth-programs/resources
- *Become mentors.* Your children can become mentors or tutors. This can be done informally through personal connections or officially through their schools. This doesn't have to be on an academic level, although it certainly can be if your children are young math or history whizzes. A mentor can simply provide support and guidance and act as a positive role model for younger children.
- *Visit nursing homes.* Have your children make cards or treats and deliver them to a local nursing home, or just visit! Kids can make a huge impact by just spending time reading, talking, or playing games with the residents.
- *Help a local family.* Contact your local church or social services office and ask if there's a local family in need who can use help. If it's during the holidays, your family can bring over gifts or holiday meals or help decorate their house. During the other months in the year, the family may be in need of the basic essentials, such as clothes, food, and household supplies.
- *Start a class project.* There's no better way to engage kids than by making them the leader. Help your children set up a donation jar or coat/food drive in their classroom. They can make signs and flyers and recruit volunteers.

THE SHARING JAR

Once your children understand the importance of charity and are incorporating it in their daily activities, giving financially will make sense to them.

In Chapter 8 you set up the three piggy banks; time to put the Share Jar to good use! As discussed in early chapters, there are plenty of views on how much to allocate to saving and sharing. There's no right or wrong answer here. What's most important is that children learn that they have to save and share some of their money. Again, they are building a habit so that, as they grow to adults, they will naturally save and share their money . . . because they always have.

An easy rule of thumb is to donate 10% of everything your children "make" to the Share Jar. This includes allowance, earned money from extra chores around the house, and gift money. This is a good starting point because they won't feel like all their money is being taken away from them but it's enough to add weight to the Share Jar. For example, if your children get $5 each week for allowance, $0.50 goes straight into the Share Jar. Another easy option is to split everything they get evenly between the three jars.

And let your children know that giving "financially" doesn't always need to be in the form of cold hard cash. It can include things like a canned goods drive (food that we buy for people we don't know) or a winter items drive (maybe they spend money to repair an old coat or buy a new one to donate). Spending money on things for people is similar to donating the cash—it's all about learning the importance of sharing.

CHILDREN-FRIENDLY CHARITIES

Donating to charity may be best understood by children if they can relate to the organization or can actually see the difference their money makes. There are countless worthy charities that children can donate to; below are just a few that are especially children friendly.

- *DonorsChoose.org* connects teachers in high-need communities with donors who want to help. Donors can search projects and choose the one they want to support. Once the project is completed, donors get a thank-you letter from the teacher as well as photos from the classroom. www.donorschoose.org
- *World Wildlife Fund*. Have animal-loving children? Visit WWF for ways that your children can donate. They can adopt their favorite animal, such as the African elephant or a sloth, or even buy toys and gifts

on the website, with all proceeds supporting the WWF. The Wildlife Conservation Society is another great animal-centric organization for your creature-loving children to donate to. www.worldwildlife.org and www.wcs.org/

- *Local animal shelters.* If your children love dogs and cats, contact your local shelter for ways they can donate.
- *Make-A-Wish.* What better way for our kids to donate than to grant a lifelong wish for children in need? Make-A-Wish grants wishes, on average every 34 minutes, for children diagnosed with life-threatening illnesses. www.wish.org
- *Toys for Tots.* Give a gift to local children in need. Toys for Tots provides toys for less fortunate children in the community. www .toysfortots.org/
- *Local hospital.* Call your local hospital and see if they would accept gifts for their pediatric patients.
- *Ronald McDonald House* provides housing to families of children receiving treatment. Your children can make a special trip to a local McDonald's to contribute to their donation box. In addition, Ronald McDonald Houses often accept gently used toys; call your local house to see what they accept. www.rmhc.org
- *Pajama Program.* Pajama Program provides pajamas and books to help ease the nighttime for children living in poverty and shelters. Children can donate as little as $10 to give pajamas and a book to one child. www.pajamaprogram.org/
- *Alex's Lemonade Stand.* This charity raises money to fight childhood cancer. Children can hold their own lemonade stand events in their neighborhood, raising money for a great cause. www.alexslemon ade.org/
- *KaBOOM!* For as little as $10, you can help KaBOOM! change the course of a kid's life by assisting communities in providing balanced and active play to all kids. Donations go to building playgrounds, ice skating rinks, and more. www.kaboom.org
- *Watsi.* Watsi uses crowdfunding technology to fund surgeries and provide health care around the world. Children can actually meet a child who needs surgery and donate directly to his or her fund. www.watsi.org
- *Oxfam gifts.* Your children can pick a gift such as a dozen baby chicks, a goat, or water jugs to be delivered to a family or community who needs that specific item. The children can design a card to send with it and receives a thank you card in return. www.oxfamgifts.com

FUNDRAISING

Once you've identified a charity that speaks to your children, create a goal of how much you want to save. Much like the goal chart described in Chapter 9 on saving, create a chart with milestones to get them excited about how much they can save for their charity. Consider donating a match as well; for example, you'll contribute $20 for every $20 they save.

Of course for many children, saving a significant amount of money could take years. Your children should understand that any little bit they can share helps. That being said, if your children are really passionate about a specific cause and want to do more, try one of the fundraising activities below. They not only help a great cause but also reinforce the financial lessons your children are learning about business and handling money. Be sure that all marketing signage and materials clearly state that all money is going to a charity. If the organization isn't well known, include a blurb on why this charity is meaningful to your children.

- Hold a garage sale or baked goods sale where all proceeds go to charity.
- Produce a neighborhood play with other children in your area. Ask attendees to donate whatever they would like as the price of admission.
- Have a raffle in your neighborhood or community. People can pay a few dollars per raffle ticket, and the winner gets his or her house cleaned or car washed.
- Speaking of . . . car washing is always a go-to for raising money. Get a group of friends, materials, and a few huge signs to wave down neighborhood traffic.
- Sell cookbooks. Gather your friends' and family's favorite recipes and create a cookbook to sell in the community.
- Crowdfund to raise money. Fundly and GoFundMe have made it easier than ever to raise money. Crowdfunding is a fundraising method that combines the power of social media with the support of your friends and family. Your children can tell your story, upload photos and videos, and explain why you're trying to raise money. Then, you share the page via Facebook, Twitter, and e-mail.

BOOKS FOR LEARNING

- *The Giving Tree* by Shel Silverstein. Because what parent doesn't need a good cry every now and then? A true classic, this book teaches the real meaning of selflessness.

- *The Spiffiest Giant in Town* by Julia Donaldson. George the giant buys all new clothes to strut around town, but soon finds that there are things more important than having the best clothes.
- *One Hen: How a Small Loan Made a Big Difference* by Katie Smith Milway. An impactful read, especially for the older elementary aged children. *One Hen* is inspired by true events and tells the story of Kojo, a boy from Ghana who turns a small loan into a thriving farm and a livelihood for many.
- *The Invisible Boy* by Trudy Ludwig. A touching story of how a small act of kindness from a child can make a huge difference.
- *Maddi's Fridge* by Lois Brandt. It tells the story of best friends Sofia and Maddi, who live in the same neighborhood and go to the same school, but while Sofia's fridge is filled with nutritious food, Maddi's family cannot afford to fill their fridge. It covers the topic of poverty and food insecurity in an honest, sensitive, and kid-friendly way.

ONLINE RESOURCES

- *Fundraising ideas.* Bonfire.com provides over 50 ideas for fundraising for any cause. https://blog.bonfire.com/fundraising-ideas/
- *Crowdfunding.* Two of the top fundraising sites in terms of ease, cost, and popularity are Fundly (https://fundly.com/) and GoFundMe (https://www.gofundme.com/).
- *Babble* provides an even more extensive list of children-friendly charities at https://www.babble.com/baby/top-best-charities-babies-kids/
- *Causes.com.* Causes is a place where your children can discover, support, and organize campaigns, fundraisers, and petitions around the issues that affect you and your community. www.causes.com
- *Donate a Photo.* A program developed by Johnson & Johnson; for every photo you share through the Donate a Photo app, Johnson & Johnson gives US$1 to a cause you care about. www.donateaphoto.com
- *Kids Can Give Too* is a way to host a birthday party with a philanthropic twist. They work with families, charities, and party places to create a community of giving while celebrating kids' birthdays. www.kidscangivetoo.com
- *Children's Charities of America* is a coalition comprised of many of America's top charitable organizations dedicated to meeting the needs of children. Your children can find information about multiple

types of charities that help kids in different ways and how they can contribute.
http://www.childrenscharities.org

SHORT AND SWEET TAKEAWAYS

1. Teaching young children about charity not only helps others, but also promotes positive habits and self-esteem.
2. Point out your children's everyday acts of kindness as examples of giving and compassion. Explain how they are linked to charity.
3. Involve your children in your own charitable activities.
4. Get your children involved, whether it's small unstructured activities, like handing out hot cocoa on cold days, or larger charitable drives organized by your children. It all matters.

Part IV

FOR THE OVERACHIEVING KIDS (OR PARENTS) WHO WANT TO LEARN *EVEN MORE* ABOUT FINANCE!

Advanced Level: 2nd–5th Grade

11

Kiddie Economics

We learned in Chapter 4 why money is so important to us personally, but why else is money important? Strap on your seat belts . . . your children are ready for Kiddie Economics!

Money is critical to businesses so they can make products, provide services, and employ workers. Our entire country depends on the money made from people and businesses. This all boils down to simple economics: specifically, macro- and microeconomics.

You may hear these words, remember your high school economics class (which you may have tried to forget), and immediately think "Maybe I'll skim this chapter." Don't skim! Most young children's extent of understanding the importance of money is "I can buy ice cream with money." While no one would deny that ice cream is certainly important, for young children to have a full appreciation of how and why money is used, they need to understand it on a higher level.

HOW DO BUSINESSES USE MONEY?

Your children know how your family uses money, which means they have a basic understanding that businesses also use money. At least, they understand it from the consumer point of view. They understand that when they want a toy, they have to go to the toy store, give the toy store money, and the toy store then gives them a toy. The next step is to understand what happens on the other side of this transaction; how does that business use money?

Figure 11.1.   Business Cycle. *Kristen Buchholz.*

First, make sure your children know what a *business* means. A business is something that sells either goods or services to a customer. *Goods* are items you buy, such as groceries, books, cars, and toys. *Services* are actions; examples of people who provide services are housekeepers, nannies, firemen, doctors, and teachers. Each one of these examples shows something that we pay a business to provide. Sometimes, that business is just one person, like a nanny. Sometimes, that business has thousands of people working for it, like a company that makes cars. Figure 11.1 provides a simple illustration of how a business uses money.

To show your children a more relevant and detailed example, walk through Figure 11.1 again, this time using the LEGO example below:[1]

- *Get money.* Before the LEGO company does anything, it needs money to buy the materials to make the toys. One of the ways it gets money is when customers buy its toys.

- *Buy materials.* To make LEGOs the company first buys the LEGO ingredients, called ABS granules. These are teeny tiny grains of plastic that come in all colors.
- *Make the product.*

  - Trucks pick up the granules and deliver them all over the world to LEGO factories.
  - At the factories, the plastic granules are put into molding machines, which melt the plastic and then put the melted plastic into tiny brick-shaped molds, similar to tiny little ice cube trays.
  - The bricks are then decorated with faces, numbers, words, and all the other images you see on different LEGO pieces.
  - These pieces are finally packaged together into sets by machines, like the *LEGO City Hospital* and *LEGO Stormtrooper*.

- *Sell the product.* These sets are then sent to stores, where customers, like your children and their friends, pay money to buy them.

WHAT DO BUSINESSES BUY WITH THEIR MONEY?

Clearly, no one actually knows the exact extent of what LEGO has to spend to bring these genius little bricks to market, so the goal here is to help your children brainstorm.

- *Materials.* The "stuff" that is used to make a product. Besides the ABS granules, what other materials does LEGO have to buy to make and sell its toys? Examples are the molds, the boxes that the LEGOs go into, and the ink used for the labels.
- *Equipment.* Items used in the creation of a product or operations of a business. Help your children identify all of the big parts that are used over and over again to make the LEGO, like the trucks, machines, robots, and factories.
- *Labor.* This includes all the people who are used to make the product or run the business. They have to pay the people who run the machines, clean the factories, and package the sets. Don't forget about the people you actually see in the store who ring up your purchase. Going back to the chapter on why money is important to your family, explain to your children that the money paid to these people is used for their families. They use it to buy food, go on vacations, and pay for doctors' visits, the same important things that you spend money on.

BUSINESS PROFITS

Your children may now understand what a business does, but what's the point of a business? Tell your children that one of the primary goals of businesses is to make money. The businesses earn money from the goods and services they sell, which is called *revenues*. Once they pay all their expenses, like materials, factories, trucks, and labor, all the money leftover is called a *profit*. A profit is the "extra" money that they can use to either make the company better or pay money to the owners. Your children will learn more about profits and revenues in the activities below and through Figure 11.2.

Pretend Play Activity: Playing Store

Playing store is a fun activity that the kids can play on a rainy day while teaching them valuable lessons in economics and money. This is especially fun for the younger kids, but older kids enjoy it as well because they can make it as detailed and sophisticated as they want. The more people you have involved, the better, so include your whole family.

- *Setup.*
    - What kind of store is it, and what do the children want to sell? They could sell dolls, LEGOs, food, art supplies—leave it up to them. For this example, let's say they are selling action figures.
    - Set up areas for three stations: the supplier, the factory, and the store. Each area should be run by a different person. Let your children's creativity run free. They can come up with a fun shop name, design signs, and create elaborate stores and factories.
    - Give your children $20 (you can use Monopoly money or real cash!) to start his business.
    - The first station is the supplier, where the "supplier" will sell the materials to the "store owner" (you can use anything you want as the pretend materials). Set the price of the material as $5.
    - Once the "store owner" buys the material, she takes it to the factory where the "factory worker" will miraculously turn the materials into action figures. Ask your children how much they think it costs to run the factory—maybe around $2.
    - Finally, the "store owner" can sell her toys in her store. Help her set it up like a real store, with the items put nicely on display.
    - Determine the pricing strategy. One option is to look up similar items online and base the price on those. Use sticky labels to put the price on each item.

- ○ Set up a cash register (which can be a toy version or just a shoebox) and a calculator to figure out change and totals.

- *Playtime:*
  - ○ Involve the whole family by having each person play a role; then switch roles once the process is complete. Make it interesting by having "difficult" customers or suppliers. Encourage your children to play the full part of the business owner; ask them about the product and why they should buy it. Your children will naturally start to "sell" the product, which is a valuable personal and professional skill to learn throughout life.
  - ○ Buy multiple items when you "shop" so they have to do some math. For the older kids, try adding in 6% sales tax as well. (This is a good opportunity to discuss what a sales tax is and where that money goes.) Help them to calculate the change owed for each transaction, and continue to challenge them by paying with different denominations and coin combinations.
  - ○ Finally, when the store closes, help them to determine their profits by calculating the "cost of goods sold" (materials) and "equipment costs" (factory) and subtracting from the total revenue they made. For an extra challenge for the older kids, add in labor costs.

Another fun version of this activity is *pretend restaurant*. Same concept as above: Your children buy the food (materials) from the grocery store, cook them in the restaurant kitchen (factory), and serve the food to the customers. With the restaurant version, kids can get creative by designing their own menu and adding in the cost of the wait staff and cooks as well.

Real-World Activity: Garage Sale

Your children are now pros at running a business and can put their "pretend store" learnings to work with a real family garage sale. As a family, determine what you want to sell at your garage sale; then let your kids help you determine the pricing. Explain to your children that, since these are used items, they have to be priced much lower than what they would cost if they were brand new in the store.

Involve your children in the design of the sale. They can determine what can be grouped together, like all kitchen stuff on one table and all clothes on a rack on the other side. Have your children take turns with the different roles, like greeting customers, helping them find items, and manning the register. Like all activities, the more involved they are, the more engaged they will be and the more they will absorb and retain.

Real-World Activity: Lemonade Stand

The idea of the lemonade stand conjures up nostalgia in most parents as they remember summer days and simpler times. Today, the lemonade stand is still a source of summer fun for many children, however, it's also now used as a shining example of how to teach children business and financial skills. In fact, in 2007, entrepreneur Michael Holthouse created a program that uses lemonade stands to teach youth how to start, own, and operate their very own business. The name? Lemonade Day, of course (https://lemonadeday.org/). Each year in participating cities, kids have the opportunity to experience entrepreneurship by setting up their business during their cities' community-wide Lemonade Day.

The lessons the lemonade stand teaches are many. To maximize the experience, below are tips for parents to follow:

- *Involve your children in every step.* This includes picking out ingredients at the grocery store, determining the pricing, and designing the signage.
- *Come up with a marketing plan.* To make this as realistic as possible, be intentional with your efforts. Brainstorm with your children different places and times that will make the most money, such as a busy street corner (with adult supervision, of course) in town at 6 p.m., when people are getting off work.
- *Make it matter.* Consider donating some of the money earned to a charity. If you go this route, be sure to tell your customers—people love to support a good cause.
- *Use real-world business accounting.* Use the real financial terms and business accounting methods. Once you've got all the ingredients and materials needed, work out the total "cost of goods sold" (cost of all ingredients and materials) with your children. Once you've closed the shop for the day, calculate the "income" (total money earned from the stand) and then the "profits" (revenues minus cost of goods sold). See Figure 11.2 for an easy business income statement example. For the ultra-ambitious parent, feel free to add in overhead costs, like wages and depreciation.

Discussion

What did your children find most difficult? What were they the most interested in? What surprised them? What mistakes did they make? Did the customers like what they were selling? Why or why not?

Income Statement	
Income	
Total Sales	**$50**
Cost of Goods Sold	
Lemons	$20
Sugar	$6
Cups	$4
Total Cost of Goods Sold	*$30*
Overhead Expenses	
Wages	$0
Selling Expenses	$0
Total Overhead Expenses	*$0*
Total Expenses	**$30**
Net Profit (Income – Expenses)	**$20**

Figure 11.2. Example of an Income Statement. *Liz Frazier.*

WHAT IS "THE ECONOMY"?

By running their lemonade stand or managing the garage sale, your children are now officially part of the economy. The older children have probably heard the word "economy" at school or home or on TV. Explain to your children that, when people talk about an economy, it's usually referring to the economy of a country, like the United States of America. An *economy* is simply a system for managing resources to meet people's needs and wants. The study of the economy is called *economics*, and a person who studies economics is called an *economist*.

Ask them what they think of when they hear the word "economy." They probably will say that they heard the word when an adult was talking about a "good economy" or a "bad economy." So what does that mean?

- *Good economy.* Usually includes lots of good-paying jobs, businesses are making money, and the overall economy of the country is growing.
- *Bad economy.* People are losing their jobs, businesses are shutting down, and the overall economy isn't growing.

MACROECONOMICS (BIG) VERSUS MICROECONOMICS (SMALL)

Economics is divided into two parts: microeconomics and macroeconomics. The way to differentiate the two to your children is easy. Microeconomics deals with the smaller stuff (micro). Macroeconomics deals with the big stuff (macro). Well, maybe there's a little more to it.

MICROECONOMICS

Without even realizing it, your sweet and innocent young children are already masters of economics, or, more specifically, microeconomics. *Microeconomics* is the study of how people and businesses make decisions on a small scale. It looks at how a company makes its products, how much it pays for materials, and what a person decides to buy at a store. Your children have already done all of this through pretend play and real-world activities.

Explain the term *microeconomics* to your children, and discuss the types of economic activities they have already done. Some examples you can provide are through their lemonade stand: they bought materials, determined pricing, and sold to consumers.

Following are some important concepts in microeconomics (so they can impress their friends):

- *Cost of goods sold.* Your children already know this one forward and backward. Cost of goods sold (COGS) is the cost of buying or making the products that a company sells. Ask your children what this would include for the lemonade stand. Answers are lemons, sugar, pitchers, cups, cardboard signs, "store," etc.
- *Opportunity costs.* This is when you give up the benefit of one thing for another. Your children have an opportunity cost with every decision they make. When they decide to go to a movie one night, the opportunity cost is they can't play at their friends' house at the same time. Regarding the lemonade stand, you can tell them an example would be if they only had $10 to spend and they chose to spend it all on the ingredients. The opportunity cost would be that they wouldn't be able to use that $10 to buy signs and decorations for the lemonade stand.

Your children already understand *supply and demand*. Ask them what they think this means. The older ones probably can give a fairly accurate answer. *Supply* is how much you *have* of something. *Demand* is how much you *want* of something. For example, if your children have 10 cups of lemonade (it's all about the lemons today), the *supply* of lemonade is 10. If they want 10 cups of lemonade, the *demand* for lemonade is 10.

Your children are probably saying "Great, but why does this matter?" Excellent question, young ones. Tell them that this matters because the supply and demand of goods and services helps to determine price. Continuing with the lemonade stand as an example, ask your children the following questions.

Pop Quiz: Lemonade Supply and Demand

(The answers are at the end of the book on page 147.)

1. Pretend you are running a lemonade stand and you have 10 cups of lemonade left (supply). It's a really hot day, and there are 20 people standing in line who want a cup of lemonade (demand). Should you charge more or less for a cup of lemonade?
2. Let's say the next day you run the same lemonade stand, but it's a rainy day. You have 10 cups of lemonade ready to sell (again, your supply), but because it's so gross out, there are only five people who want lemonade (demand). Should you increase or decrease your price?

Supply and Demand Rules to Remember

1. If the supply increases and demand stays the same, the price will go down.
2. If the supply decreases and demand stays the same, the price will go up.
3. If the supply stays the same and demand increases, the price will go up.
4. If the supply stays the same and demand decreases, the price will go down.

MACROECONOMICS

Now, it's time to put it all together for your children. If microeconomics is the study of individual businesses and people, *macroeconomics* is the study of the whole economy, which includes all the businesses and people combined. Microeconomics may be more relatable to young children because they can actually participate in activities that make up microeconomics. Below is an example of the differences for your children.

- The amount of all the Barbie Dolls sold by Mattel in the US is a part of microeconomics.
- The amount of *all* the products sold by *all* the companies in the US is a question for macroeconomics.

THE ECONOMY IS ALWAYS CHANGING

Go back to the conversation you had with your children about a good versus a bad economy. Another way to explain this to your children is to look at the different stages the economy goes through. Explain to your children that the economies of every country are always changing. Sometimes, they are growing, which is the "good economy" you discussed earlier. At other times, the economy is shrinking, which is when they will hear the term "bad economy." There are four basic cycles the economy typically goes through, and there is no set time on how long each stage will last. For a full view of the economic cycle, see Figure 11.3.

1. An *expansion* is characterized by increasing employment, economic growth, and rising prices.
2. A *peak* is the highest point of the economic cycle, when the economy is producing at its maximum, employment is at or above full employment, and prices are high.
3. After a peak, the economy usually enters into a *contraction period*, when the economy slows, employment declines (meaning unemployment increases), and pricing pressures subside.

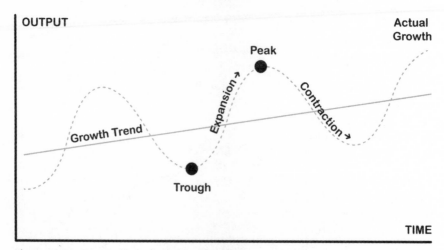

Figure 11.3.   Economic Cycle. *Kristen Buchholz.*

4. The slowing bottoms out at the *trough*, which is when the economy has hit bottom. From here, the cycle typically begins again with expansion.

Following are some important concepts in macroeconomics (so they can impress their friends even more):

- *Gross domestic product of a country (GDP)*. This is a mouthful and sounds worse than it is. Simply put, the GDP of a country is the total value of the goods and services produced by the people of that country during a specified period (usually a year). You can wow your children even more by telling them that the US GDP was over $19 trillion in 2017. To illustrate to them just how much money that is, especially when compared to other countries, show them Figure 11.4.
- *Unemployment rate*. The unemployment rate is the percentage of the labor force that is jobless. During a bad economy there are fewer jobs, so the unemployment rate can be expected to rise. When the economy is good, companies make money and hire more people, so the unemployment rate falls.
- *Inflation*. Finally, you have permission to gripe about when you were a kid it cost only $5 to go to the movies! To put it simply, explain to

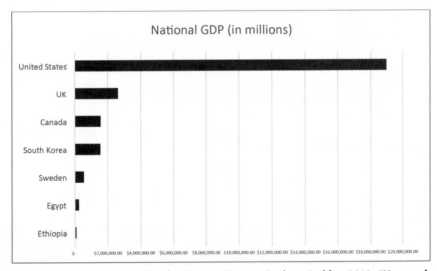

Figure 11.4.   GDP Comparison by Country. Source: Business Insider. 2018. "How each US state's economy measures up to countries around the world." Updated November 2018. https://www.businessinsider.com/how-each-us-states-economy-measures-up-to -countries-around-the-world-2018-5. *Source:* **Wikipedia. 2015. "Comparison between U.S. states and countries by GDP (nominal.)" Updated August 2018. https://en.wikipedia .org/wiki/Comparison_between_U.S._states_and_countries_by_GDP_(nominal)**

your children that inflation means the cost of products and services become more expensive over time. Tell them that the average rate of inflation in the US is about 3%. An example: This year an ice cream cone costs $1. With 3% inflation, next year it will cost $1.03. Again, your children may be saying "Why do I care?" This means that, if they get $10 for allowance, they can buy more ice cream with that $10 now than they will be able to buy in the future.

- *Economic policy.* While fascinating to a rare breed, most don't understand the ins and outs of economic policy. So don't expect your children to get this. What they need to know is the banks and government are constantly using different types of economic policies to balance and maintain a healthy economy. They can use tools to slow down the economy if it's growing too fast. They also can use these same tools to stimulate an economy that's slow. This will give your children the assurance that, when there is a bad economy, there are a lot of people working to fix it.

Pop Quiz: Macro versus Micro

Read the hypothetical scenarios below, and ask your children if they're macroeconomics or microeconomics. (The answers are at the end of the book on 148.)

1. McDonald's decides to lower the price of its Chicken McNuggets from $4.99 to $4.50.
2. Reports show that the total amount of chicken sold in the US declined by 3% over the past year.
3. Over the past four years, the cost of milk rose an average of 4%.
4. Your father raised your allowance by $2 this month.
5. Your elementary school decided to give holiday bonuses to its teachers this year.

BOOKS FOR LEARNING

- *Striker Jones: Elementary Economics for Elementary Detectives* by Maggie Larche. This is one in a series of books that follow Striker Jones and his friends on quests to solve puzzles and crimes. Striker has to use his knowledge of basic economics to solve each mystery, making this a fun and educational read.
- *How to Make an Apple Pie and See the World* by Marjorie Priceman. This is a beautiful book for all ages. A simple recipe for apple pie takes readers all over the world to find the ingredients. Great lessons illustrated in business economics.

ONLINE RESOURCES

- *Scholastic* has created a program called *Economy for Kids*, which provides resources and games about the economy that are fun and simple to understand.
  http://www.scholastic.com/browse/collection.jsp?id=455
- *Biz Kid$* provides entertaining videos and lessons tailored to kids, meant to break down complex economic terms and concepts.
  http://bizkids.com/themes/economy

MATCHING GAME: TERMS TO KNOW

Table 11.1. Matching Game: Terms to Know

Match each of these important terms to its correct definition.

Business	The "stuff" that is used to make a product.
Goods	The cost of buying or making the products that a company sells during a period.
Services	When you give up the benefit of one thing for another.
Materials	An operation that sells either goods or services to a customer.
Equipment	The study of how business and people make decisions at a small scale.
Labor	How much you *want* of something.
Economy	The percentage of the labor force that is jobless.
Microeconomics	Items you buy, such as groceries, books, cars, and toys.
Macroeconomics	The total value of the goods and services produced by the residents of that country during a specified period (usually a year).
Cost of goods sold (COGS)	A system for allocating resources to meet people's needs and wants.
Opportunity cost	How much you *have* of something.
Supply	Items used in the creation of a product or for the operation of a business.
Demand	The study of the whole economy, which includes all of the business and people together.
Gross domestic product (GDP)	Actions that are sold. Examples are housekeepers, nannies, firemen, doctors, and teachers.
Unemployment rate	All of the people who are used to make the product or run the business.

SHORT AND SWEET TAKEAWAYS

1. Businesses use money too. Next time you buy a toy for your children, explain that the store uses the money you spend to buy the materials needed to make more toys. The money left over after all expenses are paid is called profits.
2. Economics is the study of how goods and services are exchanged. Microeconomics studies how individual people and businesses use money. Macroeconomics studies how all the people and businesses combined use money.

NOTE

1. LEGO. n.d. "How LEGOBricks are made." Accessed September 3, 2018. https://www.lego.com/en-us/service/help/bricks-building/brick-facts/how-lego-bricks-are-made-408100000007834.

12

Introduction to Banking and Investing

Once your children's piggy bank starts overflowing and they have a solid understanding of money, it's a good time to start learning more complex saving concepts, such as interest, banking, and investing. Keep in mind that these are sophisticated subjects that many adults don't even get, so go easy on yourself. This chapter will help you break down these concepts into manageable pieces so your children can relate to them.

INTEREST: MONEY MAKING MONEY

The *Saving for a Goal* activity in Chapter 9 deliberately left out the interest factor. That activity was meant to be an introduction to savings, and it's important to focus on teaching your children one thing at a time so they are not overwhelmed. The next time they are ready to save for something, repeat the activity and include interest. They will welcome the addition of interest because it will help them reach their goal faster.

Explain to your children that, when you put your money in a savings account at a bank, the bank can actually borrow that money to give to other customers. Tell them not to worry; their money is completely safe in the bank, and they will get it all back whenever they want it. But in return for letting the bank borrow their money, the bank will pay them *interest*, which is a percentage of the total amount of money in the account, paid over a certain amount of time. This is the same concept as the interest a credit card charges you (Chapter 13), but this time the bank is the borrower. How much interest the consumer will make depends on three things:

1. *The amount of the "loan."* The more they have in the account, the more interest they make.
2. *The interest rate.* The higher the interest rate, the more money they will make.
3. *The length of time in the account.* The longer the money is in the account, the more money they will make.

Real-World Activity: Paying Interest

This is a lot for children to absorb, and it still feels too hypothetical for children to truly understand. Make it real for them by paying them interest on their Save Jar. In the beginning it may seem just like a magical gift from the interest fairy. Over time, they will start to see that the amount of interest they get corresponds to how much they have saved, which will be an incentive to save even more.

- Start with 10% interest because that's the easiest amount to calculate.
- At the end of each month, count up the money in their Save Jar together, and add 10%. Tell them that this is the special "Piggy Bank" interest rate and most interest rates are lower (otherwise, they will be sorely disappointed when they actually start investing and get a measly 7% return).
- You can show them how to calculate with simple math the 10% they will earn. If they have $15.00 in their account, move the decimal to the left one space, equaling $1.50 in interest earned. Same thing if they have $61.54 in their account; the interest will be $6.15.

FUN WITH CALCULATORS (YES, FUN!)

Yes, you read that correctly . . . *fun!* Around third grade, when kids are learning more challenging math lessons in school, show them a simple online savings calculator like one of those listed below. If you have younger children with strong math skills, they too could be ready for some calculator fun.

These calculators allow the user to play with all the different interest variables listed above to see how the results change. Try out different scenarios with your children, such as a longer time period or depositing less or more money each month. Let them run wild with it (as wild as one can get with a calculator). This is a great tool to illustrate the power of starting early and earning interest.

- *Bankrate.* https://www.bankrate.com/calculators/savings/simple-savings-calculator.aspx

- *NerdWallet.* https://www.nerdwallet.com/blog/banking/savings
  -calculator/
- *MSN Money* (this calculator is great because it includes a chart showing exactly how much you have over time). https://www.msn.com/
  en-us/money/tools/savingscalculator

Another way to illustrate to your children how interest works is with an
interest chart, shown in Table 12.1. This gives them a visual overview of
the amount of money earned with different interest rates.

Table 12.1. Interest Calculations

Beginning Amount	Monthly Deposit	Interest (Annual)	Number of Years	Final Savings
$100	$0	2%	10 years	$122
$100	$0	6%	10 years	$179
$100	$0	12%	10 years	$311

Once they are comfortable with the basics of the calculator and interest
rates, give them specific problems to figure out. Example: How can you
save up $100,000? There are endless combinations that will get them to
$100,000. Several scenarios are listed in Table 12.2.

Table 12.2. Savings Calculations

Beginning Amount	Monthly Deposit	Interest (Annual)	Number of Years	Final Savings (Rounded)
$1	$1,000	5%	7 years	$100K
$10	$85	7%	30 years	$100K
$2,000	$500	9%	10 years	$100K

Pop Quiz: Interest(ing) Math

Use the quick quiz below to gauge your children's understanding of saving and interest and to use as a discussion starter. (The answers are at the
end of the book on page 148.)

1. How much interest will you earn in one month with a 10% interest
   rate and $23.20 saved?
   a. $232
   b. $6
   c. $2.32
   d. $.23

2. Sara's piggy bank earns 15% interest, and John's piggy bank earns 5% interest. If they both have $10 in their piggy banks this month, who will have more next month?

    a. Sara
    b. John
    c. They will have the same amount.

3. Tyler wants a new scooter. He has $40 in his Save Jar, and the scooter costs $71.50. How much more money does he need to save before he can buy the scooter?

    a. $71.50
    b. $40
    c. $60
    d. $31.50

THE BUSINESS OF BANKING

Although a simple piggy bank will suffice with younger children, around third grade (or whenever the piggy is about to burst), your children may be ready to upgrade to a real bank. Most banks will allow young children to open an account jointly with their parents. Children under the age of 18 must have their parents or legal guardians named as joint account holders. Being the joint account holder means that the parents and children both have equal rights and access to the account so you can manage and control the finances while they are young. Opening an account with your children is a great way to teach them about the basics of banking and solidify their understanding of interest, which can lead up to investing.

WHAT IS A BANK?

Before opening an account, tell your children that, because they have done such a great job of saving in their Save Jar, it's time to move their savings into a real bank. Tell them a *bank* is an institution that does several things, including:

1. Keeps money safe in a bank account
2. Pays interest on the money in their bank account
3. Lends people money for expensive purchases, like buying a house. The bank then charges them interest on that money.

BANK ACCOUNTS

Tell your children that, after you go to the bank to open up an account, you have to make a *deposit*, which means they give the bank money to add to their account. There are two primary types of accounts that they need to understand at this point.

1. *Checking account.* They can think of the checking account like their Spend Jar. This is the money they will use on everyday purchases.
2. *Savings account.* This is obviously like their Save Jar. They hold money here when they want to save it and earn interest.

OPENING A BANK ACCOUNT

First things first. Time to count your children's loot. Remember before there were machines that counted money for you? Take a trip back in time and help your children roll all their money into coin wrappers. (Go ahead and play a CD or VHS while you're in a nostalgic mood.)

Once you have all the coins organized, bring your children with you to open the account. Explain to the bank representative that this is their first bank account and you are teaching them about saving and banking. Ask if they can give your children a tour of the bank and explain the different processes. Here's what to look for when opening an account:

- No monthly fees or minimum balance requirements.
- A local branch that you can visit with your children so they can see how a bank works firsthand.
- Interest rates. Savings rates are typically very low, but compare banks. Even if it's low, you will still be able to show your children that their money is growing.
- Ask if there are any special accounts or programs for children.

HOW DO I GET MY MONEY?

Your children may be thinking "This all sounds great, but all my money will be in this big building now?" Explain to them that getting money out of the bank is simple by using these methods.

- *Checks.* This is close to becoming old-fashioned, but show your children a check (if you still have them!). Explain that you can write in any amount, give someone the check, and that person then takes the check to the bank and exchanges it for money. Get checks for their account, even though they may be too young to use them yet.

- *Debit cards.* Many people feel uncomfortable giving their children a debit card because it looks like a credit card and it's not the way they paid for things when they were younger. Somehow, it just *feels* wrong. However, today debit cards are one of the most frequently used forms of payment and are the equivalent of cash.

  We started with cash and coins because seeing and touching money is the best way for them to learn. Once they have the basics, you can move on to more practical applications. You can get your young children a debit card because you will maintain full control of it while they are young. While cash may still be the primary way they use money at this point, you can keep their card in your wallet and help them use it occasionally when they want to make purchases.

- *ATM.* Tell your children that they will get an ATM card, which usually is also a debit card. They can put it in an ATM (automated teller machine), enter in a secret passcode, and get money from their accounts. If they are going somewhere without you where they need to bring cash, such as a school trip, visit the ATM together to withdraw the money for them.

BANK STATEMENTS

Each month when the banking statement arrives, whether online or in the mail, review it with your children. A seven-year-old does not need to understand *all the details* (nor do most adults), so skip the terms and conditions. Show them the following.

1. How much money they had at the beginning of the month
2. How much they deposited/withdrew
3. How much they have now at the end of the month

Point out if they have more or less money in their account than last month and why. If it's a savings account, show them that they earned money through interest (yes, it will probably be only $.0013, but at least it's something!). This leads to a discussion on investing.

INVESTING

Once again, we are not trying to create the youngest Warren Buffett here (although no one would complain if Junior followed in his footsteps).

Investing gets very complicated very quickly, so keep it simple and stick to the basics.

Begin by explaining to them that besides savings accounts, there are other ways their money can earn money. One way is through *investing*, which means spending money in the hopes of making more money. They are already investing by depositing money into their savings account because they are earning money from it. Another way to invest is by purchasing stocks. Below is a script you can use (and feel free to replace Disney with your children's favorite store).

> You know all those stuffed animals you have upstairs? They were all made by a company called Disney. Disney needs money to make all those toys. We already discussed how they make money by selling stuffed animals. Another way they get money is by selling stock. When someone buys their stock, it means they own a little piece of Disney Company.

WHAT IN THE WORLD IS A STOCK?

When your children ask this question, tell them a *stock* is a piece of paper (real or virtual) that represents ownership in a company. Each share of stock is worth a certain percentage of the company.

For example, if a company has 100 total shares of stock, then each share of stock represents 1% of the company. If your children own 10 shares, they own 10% of the company. Companies sell stock to raise money for their company so they can buy materials, create new products, buy new factories, or pay their employees. Remind them how they had to buy materials and spend money on their business during the activities in Chapter 11. Big companies may have billions of stock. People then buy and sell stocks through a place called the *stock market*.

WHY DO PEOPLE BUY STOCKS?

Similar to putting money in their savings accounts, people buy stock in companies to try to make more money. They are letting the company borrow their money, and in return the company is paying them interest. If the company does well, the price of the stock increases, and the people who own stock make money. If a company doesn't do well, the people who own the stock lose money.

Give them an example of a company they know, like Hershey's. Let's say they bought one stock of Hershey's and the stock cost $100 when they bought it.

- *Scenario 1.* The week after they bought the stock, Hershey's came out with a new chocolate bar . . . the most delicious chocolate bar anyone has ever tasted, even putting Willy Wonka to shame. Everyone wanted one, and the company made a ton of money selling the bars. People see the company is doing well and buy stock, which makes the stock price go up (remind them of supply and demand in Chapter 11). The stock is now worth $120, so if they sold their stock they would make $20 profit because they paid only $100 and sold it for $120!
- *Scenario 2.* Now, explain the flip side. This time, Hershey's still made a new chocolate bar, but instead of tasting delicious, people said it tasted like they were eating out of a garbage can. Hershey's lost money because no one bought their "garbage can" bars. The people who own their stock see that the company is not doing well, so they want to sell before they lose their money. The stock of Hershey's goes down because the demand for the stock has decreased. The stock is now worth only $80. Since your children bought the stock for $100, if they sold it now they would get only $80, meaning they would lose $20.

Full disclosure: Your children will not completely understand this, and that's okay; most adults don't fully grasp the stock market. This is just an introduction to the ideas and terms around investing. You can continue this as an ongoing conversation by working it into their daily routine.

If your children love their shoes, tell them a company called Nike makes them. This goes for Disney, Coca-Cola, McDonald's, Mattel, and so on. This gets them thinking about the companies behind the products they use and the reasons these companies may succeed or fail.

Real-World Activity: Invest!

One way to teach your children how to invest in the stock market is to invest in the stock market! Yes, your young children can invest in the market without needing to understand the meaning of an ETF (electronic funds transfer), and they don't need to start with a lot of money. If they can use an app, they can invest.

Many companies have recently recognized the need to teach children about investing but saw that there was no simple real-world way to teach them. Stockpile is an example of a company that developed programs designed specifically for kids. By learning investment basics at a young age, they won't be intimidated by more complex investment concepts as they get older. Plus, they will be more comfortable with the risk associated with investing. Below is a list of several digital tools and apps that allow your children to invest in a safe and simple way.

- *Stockpile.* Download the free Stockpile app, sign up for an account, deposit money, and buy a stock. Sounds like most other trading platforms; however, the beauty of this app is you can spend however much you want by purchasing fractional shares. If you want your children to invest only $25, you can buy 0.25 shares of Disney. The app is designed with kids in mind, so it's easy for them to log on and watch their stock go up and down.
  https://www.stockpile.com/
- *Robinhood.* Robinhood was created to make investing as simple as possible. That being said, it was designed with millennials in mind, not kids. The parents will need to help their children with the app. However, the major advantage of this app is there are no fees and no account minimums. It costs nothing if you and your children want to try it out.
  https://robinhood.com/
- *The Stock Market Game.* The Stock Market Game is an online simulation of the market for kids in grades 4–12. Although designed for a classroom environment, parents can use this resource with their children to learn the basics of investing without actually spending any money.
  https://www.stockmarketgame.org/

You can also "play the market" through pretend games. You don't have to be fancy. Tell them to choose a stock; then create a pretend "stock certificate" for them (see Figure 12.1 for an example). Record how much it cost; then using simple search engines like Google or Yahoo Finance, track the stock price each week, and calculate how much your children have.

For example, if your children buy one share of Nike at $70 and after three weeks the stock is at $78, your children have earned $8 ($78 – $70). Same goes for when the price drops. If the stock is bought at $70 and then goes down to $65, your children lost $5. If the stock price increases or decreases dramatically, research with your children what may have happened to cause the change in price.

Pretend Play: Stock Market Game

This is similar to the activity above, but make it a group competition with your children's friends or your family. Choose 10 stocks of companies they are familiar with, like Apple, Disney, or Nike. Everyone gets $100 (pretend) and chooses one of those stocks to "invest" it in. For one month, check the stock prices each week, and record how much money each person has. Get the group together weekly to compare earnings and discuss why the stocks are moving. This can be a fun family dinner activity and

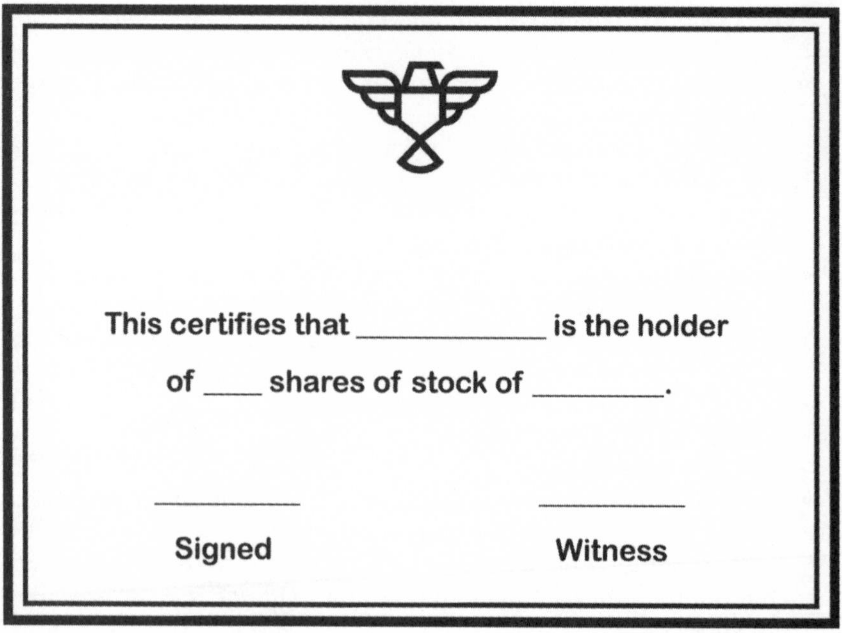
This certifies that ___________ is the holder

of ___ shares of stock of _______.

Signed Witness

Figure 12.1. Stock Certificate Example. ***Kristen Buchholz.***

gives you yet another chance to explain investing. Make it a competition with a prize for whoever has the most money at the end.

MATCHING GAME: TERMS TO KNOW

Table 12.3. Matching Game: Terms to Know

Match each of these important terms to its correct definition.	
Bank	A method of payment where the amount is written on a form and the payee can exchange it for money at a bank.
Deposit	Spending money with the hopes of making money.
Checks	A percentage of the total amount of money in the account paid over a certain amount of time.
Interest	A tool used by companies to raise money and represents ownership in that company.
Investing	The institution where stocks are bought and sold.
Stock	An institution that keeps money safe, pays interest on money in accounts, and lends people money.
Stock market	The money you give to the bank to put into an account.

SHORT AND SWEET TAKEAWAYS

1. Money can earn money. If your children let a bank "borrow" their money, the bank will pay them extra money called interest.
2. A bank is an institution where people store their money. It keeps money safe, pays interest, and lends money to people. Opening a savings and checking account for your children allows them to learn about real-world financial transactions firsthand.
3. Your children can also put their money to work by investing. One way to invest is to buy stock in a company. Stock represents ownership in a company. When a company does well/poor, stock owners do well/poor.

13

Learning about Advertising, Debt, and Taxes

Time for a giant dose of reality for your kids. Until now, your children have been learning about the fun side of finance (Right!? Saving, economics, working—the fun stuff!). Unfortunately, there's a darker side too—and it goes by the name of debt, advertising, and yes . . . taxes. The goal isn't to scare your children or taint their rosy view of finance, but it's important that they are aware of these concepts.

ADVERTISING

These days it's especially important to teach your children about advertising. Companies are getting smarter and have become experts at using data to target anyone and everyone. Children are especially vulnerable to this. How many times have your children seen an ad on TV and said they *had to have* the product advertised?

Next time this happens, remind them of the lessons on microeconomics in Chapter 11. Explain to your children that the company that makes that toy wants them to buy it. Every time someone buys one of the toys, that company makes money. This means that they will say anything to make people want to buy it. They may say it's the fastest, best, prettiest, or coolest toy ever, but that doesn't mean it's true. Help your children understand that they have to decide on their own if they want to buy something and advertising shouldn't influence their decision.

ELECTRONIC PAYMENTS

Even though your children aren't using electronic payment systems yet, they see you use them every day. For now, there's no need to sit down and explain each type of payment option to your children. Instead, next time you use your card or make a payment online, explain it to your children using these simple definitions.

- *Debit cards.* When you pay with a debit card, it's just like paying with cash. The card machine takes that money from the parent's bank account and puts it into the store's bank account.
- *Credit cards.* When people pay with credit cards, they are borrowing money that they don't have. They have to pay this money back, plus pay extra money called interest. *Interest* is what the credit card companies charge you to let you borrow their money. Your children aren't old enough to be targeted by credit card companies, but start discouraging their use early.

DEBT: THE GOOD, THE BAD, AND THE VERY UGLY

Your children are thankfully way too young to actually accumulate any debt at this point, but it's never too early to start talking about the dangers. Debt is money borrowed that must be repaid, with interest. There are two primary types of debt: loans and credit cards.

- *Credit cards.* If credit card companies had their way, they would allow children to open a credit card before their first birthday. Luckily (for now), children must be 18 before they get their own card. Although this seems like a long time from now, start talking to them about it now so they are ready to make smart decisions later.

    Explain to your children that, when they get older (as in, the second they turn 18), companies will start to offer them credit cards. This may be through the mail, on college campus, by phone, at the mall, on the plane . . . OK, really anywhere they go. Below are the primary card features to explain to your children.

    - ○ *Credit limit.* This is how much money you have available to spend. It could be $500, or it could be in the thousands of dollars. The danger here is that it feels like "extra" or "free" money. However, it is anything but free.
    - ○ *Balance.* How much money you've spent on the card. If you used your credit card to buy $50 worth of gummy bears and $50 on M&Ms, your balance would be $100 (and you would probably be

sick to your stomach!). This is how much you owe the credit card company and are expected to pay back.

- ○ *Available credit.* The credit limit minus the balance.
- ○ *Interest rate.* As mentioned, interest is what the credit card company charges you to let you borrow its money. How much interest you have to pay is based on the interest rate, which is a percentage of the balance. If your balance is $100 and the interest rate is 20%, the interest you owe is $20 (don't worry if your children don't know what percentages are yet; they just need to understand that they will have to pay interest). So they spent $100, but now they owe $120. The takeaway is, the lower the interest rate, the better.
- ○ *Minimum payment.* The amount you have to pay back each month.

- • *Loans.* Loans are usually used for large one-time purchases and are paid back over a specific amount of time. There are several types of loans that your children may have already heard about.

  - ○ *Student loans.* Your children should understand that college is *expensive* and most don't have the money to pay for it. Either the parents or the children have to borrow money to pay for it.
  - ○ *Mortgage loan.* Tell your children that buying a home is probably the biggest item they will ever buy. Like school, most people don't have that much money lying around, so they have to borrow it from a bank.

RULES OF DEBT

Debt can be a helpful money management tool when used responsibly. Unfortunately, many don't understand the dangers of debt. While your children won't fully grasp this, you can at least expose them and get them started on the right path. With any type of debt, your children should understand the following rules.

1. Compare interest rates. This is especially true for credit cards. The lower the interest rate, the less money you will have to pay.
2. Is the debt "worth it"? If you borrow money for a house, you now own a house that your family can live in. If you borrow money for school, you get a great education and probably a better job. Make sure that whatever you are borrowing money for is important enough to pay the extra interest.
3. Use credit cards only for emergencies. If you don't have cash for a purchase, you can't afford it.
4. Don't borrow more than you can afford.

TAXES

This topic is at the end of the chapter for a reason. You are not an accountant. Your children are not accountants. Unless they specify that their dream is to be an accountant, it's assumed they will probably hire someone to do their taxes later in life (or use a program, such as TurboTax). So you don't need to get into the details of mortgage interest deductions right now with your children. At a high level, *tax* is an amount of money individuals and organizations must pay to their government. Children need to know the basics: why we pay taxes, where taxes go, and how much we pay.

The "Why"

Rarely is there an adult who celebrates paying taxes. We work hard for our money only to see up to half of it disappear in the IRS black hole. With that out of the way, no matter how a parent personally feels about taxes, the law states that we have to pay them. When explaining taxes to your children, you can acknowledge that it can be frustrating, but try to focus on the positives.

> The money paid in taxes goes to the salaries of workers, such as judges, police, and firefighters. It also helps to ensure the roads you travel on are safe and well maintained. Taxes fund many schools, public libraries, and parks as well as government programs that help the poor and less fortunate.

Next time you're at a playground with your children, explain that the reason they have this playground is because everyone pays taxes and the town decided to use some of that money to build a playground.

The "Where"

The majority of our taxes go to the federal government. This money is split between many programs. Some goes to programs to help others, like Social Security and Medicare. Federal money also goes toward the US military to help keep the people in this country safe. What's not allocated to the federal government is split between state and local governments for things such as transportation, hospitals, education, retirement, and health care.

The "How Much"

Tell your children that people pay a percentage of how much money they make for taxes and that percentage depends on how much money they make in total. The more money they make, the higher the percentage is.

As employees, their employers will automatically withhold some money from each paycheck to send to the IRS.

Around April 15 of each year, everyone files their taxes, which is a process to record income, expenses, and other information to establish how much tax they owe the previous year. They then either get a refund or owe more money. How much tax they pay in total will depend on many variables, and to calculate that, most people will need the help of a professional or a service like Quicken.

Wait. Do My Children Have to Pay Taxes?

The short and clear answer is *maybe*. More than likely at this age, your children's income is coming from self-employment (mowing lawns, washing cars, etc.). For tax purposes, your children would be treated as self-employed, meaning that they would be required to file a tax return and pay a 15.3% self-employment tax when income exceeds $400. Although the idea of filing taxes for your nine-year-old is probably giving you a headache, try to view it as a positive. You are teaching your children (in an all-too-real way) about taxes. Plus, if they are having to pay taxes, that means they are making a lot of money!

MATCHING GAME: TERMS TO KNOW

Table 13.1.   Matching Game: Terms to Know

Match each of these important terms to its correct definition.

Debit card	A payment method where you borrow money that has to be repaid.
Tax	A payment method similar to cash.
Credit card	A percentage of money that is paid over time, based on how much money is borrowed.
Interest	An amount of money individuals and organizations must pay to their government.

SHORT AND SWEET TAKEAWAYS

1. Your children are way too young to have any debt, but it's the perfect time to teach them about it! Be sure your children understand that, when you borrow money, you have to repay it, plus pay a fee.
2. Explain to your children the importance of paying taxes and where that money goes. When they inevitably ask questions that leave you stumped, tell them there are smart people called accountants who can answer those questions for them when they get older.

14

Some Parting Words

Congratulations! You should be proud of your children for all they've accomplished. You should also be especially proud of yourself for all you've taught. You, singlehandedly, have changed the way this next generation thinks, feels, and interacts with money. If that's not impressive, then what is?

Your children are now starting their young lives with a solid understanding of saving, responsible spending, how to avoid debt, and the importance of giving back. This valuable knowledge will be used throughout their childhoods and into their adult years, enabling them to make smart decisions and live financially healthy and independent lives.

Remember, although the book is done, this is a journey, not a destination. Continue the conversations with your children, and they will continue to expand their knowledge as they get older. Stay positive when talking with your children about money. Keep in mind that money is neither good nor bad; it's simply a tool to help you reach your goals. Keep them engaged by letting them manage their own money, make their own financial decisions, and then learn from their successes and failures.

I'm looking forward to seeing what our children can do.

Appendix A

Matching Game Answers

CHAPTER 6

Match each of these important terms to its correct definition.

Needs	The things that are essential or important to your survival.
Wants	The things that are nice to have, but you can live without.
Priorities	The things that are most important.
Credit card	A payment method where you borrow money that has to be repaid.

CHAPTER 11

Match each of these important terms to its correct definition.

Business	An operation that sells either goods or services to a customer.
Goods	Items you buy, such as groceries, books, cars, and toys.
Services	Actions that are sold. Examples are housekeepers, nannies, firemen, doctors, and teachers.
Materials	The "stuff" that is used to make a product.
Equipment	Items used in the creation of a product or for the operation of a business.

Labor	All the people who are used to make the product or run the business.
Economy	A system for allocating resources to meet people's needs and wants.
Microeconomics	The study of how business and people make decisions at a small scale.
Macroeconomics	The study of the whole economy, which includes all of the business and people together.
Cost of goods sold (COGS)	The cost of buying or making the products that a company sells during a period.
Unemployment rate	The percentage of the labor force that is jobless.
Opportunity cost	When you give up the benefit of one thing for another.
Gross domestic product (GDP)	The total value of the goods and services produced by the residents of that country during a specified period (usually a year).
Supply	How much you *have* of something.
Demand	How much you *want* of something.

CHAPTER 12

Match each of these important terms to its correct definition.

Bank	An institution that keeps money safe, pays interest on money in accounts, and lends people money.
Deposit	The money you give to the bank to put into an account.
Checks	A method of payment where the amount is written on a form and the payee can exchange it for money at a bank.
Interest	A percentage of the total amount of money in the account paid over a certain amount of time.
Investing	Spending money with the hopes of making money.
Stock	A tool used by companies to raise money and represents ownership in that company.
Stock market	The institution where stocks are bought and sold.

CHAPTER 13

Match each of these important terms to its correct definition.

Debit card   A payment method similar to cash.

Interest   A percentage of money that is paid over time, based on how much money is borrowed.

Taxes   An amount of money individuals and organizations must pay to their government.

Credit card   A payment method where you borrow money that has to be repaid.

Appendix B

Quiz Answers

CHAPTER 3: POP QUIZ—PUT YOUR COIN COUNTING TO THE TEST

1. What are three ways to make $.63?
   ANSWER: Many correct answers.

2. a. How can you make $.37 using four coins?
   ANSWER: 1 quarter, 1 dime, and 2 pennies

   b. What about using 7 coins?
   ANSWER: 2 dimes, 3 nickels, and 2 pennies

   c. Try one more time using 11 coins.
   ANSWER: 2 dimes, 2 nickels, and 7 pennies

3. What's worth more: 1 quarter, 3 dimes, and 5 pennies or 17 pennies and 1 dime?
   ANSWER: 1 quarter, 3 dimes, and 5 pennies

4. How many nickels are in 2 quarters?
   ANSWER: 10 nickels

CHAPTER 3: POP QUIZ—HIDDEN OBJECTS

After your children have looked at the images and numbers on the bills, tell them that there are multiple "hidden" symbols and pictures on each bill. Have them find the answers to the questions below.

1. Where is the eyeball?
   ANSWER: Back of the $1 bill, on top of the pyramid.

2. Find the eagle on each bill.
3. Which bill doesn't have an eagle on the front?
   ANSWER: The $1 bill.

4. How many times can you find the number 13 on the $1 bill?
   ANSWER: There are 13 arrows, 13 olive branch leaves, 13 olive fruits, 13 stars above the eagle, 13 steps of the pyramid, and 13 bars on the shield.

5. Which bill has the White House on the back?
   ANSWER: The $20 bill.

6. Find the man sitting in a chair.
   ANSWER: Back of the $5 bill, Abraham Lincoln statue.

7. Find the hidden keys.
   ANSWER: On the front of each bill.

8. Which bill has a torch on the front?
   ANSWER: The $10 bill.

CHAPTER 9: POP QUIZ—SAVE OR SPEND JAR

Give your children examples of different items and ask if they would use the money from their Save or Spend Jar. For the Save Jar items, help them come up with a plan on how they could save for it. Remember, at this stage it's not meant to be perfect or exact. These examples are simple, but they are meant to be simple. The goal is to introduce these concepts to them so they start *thinking about saving* and become comfortable with the concept. A few examples that you can ask your children are below, but you can use anything relevant to your children. Start off by telling them they have $10 in their Spend Jar and $20 in their Save Jar.

1. You are at the grocery store and see the cutest stuffed animal unicorn. You have to have it, and the price is $4. Does this come out of your Spend Jar or Save Jar?
   ANSWER: Spend

2. You are with your parents at the arcade and want to play one more game, but your parents say you have to use your own money. Each game costs $2. Does this come out of your Save Jar or Spend Jar?
   ANSWER: Spend

3.   a. You are at your friend's house who has the most amazing remote-controlled airplane. You tell your dad you want the same one; together you look up the price, which is $40. Which jar will this come out of? (Help your children think through this question until you determine that they don't have enough money in their Spend Jar so this is something they will need to save for.)

   b. The second part of this question is to then come up with a plan. They have $20 in their Save Jar. They get $9/week in allowance and put $3 in the Save Jar each week. How long will it take until they have saved up enough money?
   ANSWER: It will take them about seven weeks until they have $40 for the airplane ($40 − $20 = $20; then, divide $20 by 3).

   c. If that seems like a long time to them, walk through ways they could save more, such as doing odd jobs around the house to earn extra money or putting more money in the Save Jar and less in the Spend Jar. Or they could allocate money meant for the Spend Jar toward the airplane.

CHAPTER 11: POP QUIZ—LEMONADE SUPPLY AND DEMAND

1. Pretend you are running a lemonade stand and you have 10 cups of lemonade left (supply). It's a really hot day, and there are 20 people standing in line who want a cup of lemonade (demand). Should you charge more or less for a cup of lemonade?
   ANSWER: You should increase the price. If the demand is higher than the supply, there will be a shortage of lemonade, meaning you don't have enough. When you raise the price, you may sell less because it's more expensive, but you will make a higher profit on each cup.

2. Let's say the next day you run the same lemonade stand, but it's a rainy day. You have 10 cups of lemonade ready to sell (again, your supply), but because it's so gross out, there are only five people who want lemonade (demand). Should you increase or decrease your price?
   ANSWER: You should decrease the price. If the supply is higher than the demand, then there is a surplus of lemonade, meaning you have too much. Once you lower the price, even though your profit will be lower per cup, you will sell more cups of lemonade.

CHAPTER 11: POP QUIZ—MACRO VERSUS MICRO

Read the hypothetical scenarios below, and ask your children if they're
macroeconomics or microeconomics.

1. McDonald's decides to lower the price of its Chicken McNuggets
   from $4.99 to $4.50.
   ANSWER: Microeconomics, because it's dealing with one specific
   business.

2. Reports show that the total amount of chicken sold in the US declined by 3% over the past year.
   ANSWER: Macroeconomics, because it's looking at supply and demand over multiple businesses throughout the whole country.

3. Over the past four years, the cost of milk rose an average of 4%.
   ANSWER: Macroeconomics, because it's looking at inflation over an
   entire category.

4. Your father raised your allowance by $2 this month.
   ANSWER: Microeconomics, because it's looking at the income of
   one person.

5. Your elementary school decided to give holiday bonuses to its teachers this year.
   ANSWER: Microeconomics, because it's looking at the wages for
   one business (the school).

CHAPTER 12: POP QUIZ—INTEREST(ING) MATH

Use the quick quiz below to gauge your children's understanding of saving and interest and to use as a discussion starter.

1. How much interest will you earn in one month with a 10% annual
   interest rate and $23.20 saved?
   ANSWER: $2.32

2. Sara's piggy bank earns 15% interest, and John's piggy bank earns
   5% interest. If they both have $10 in their piggy banks this month,
   who will have more next month?
   ANSWER: Sara

3. Tyler wants a new scooter. He has $40 in his Save Jar, and the scooter
   costs $71.50. How much more money does he need to save before he
   can buy the scooter?
   ANSWER: $31.50

Appendix C
Activity Index

CHAPTER 3

CHAPTER 4

CHAPTER 5

CHAPTER 6

CHAPTER 12

CHAPTER 13

About the Author

Liz Frazier is a certified financial planner specializing in financial planning for families and working professionals. She decided to go into financial planning after the birth of her first child because, like so many other new parents, she realized the overwhelming need to make sure her family was financially prepared and protected. Her goal is to alleviate the anxiety that surrounds finances and provide simple and painless advice for all of life's stages and changes.

Her passion for teaching children finance began soon after she started her practice. She realized how intimidated most people were about finance—for good reason! They had never been exposed to it, so of course they weren't comfortable with it. She realized that if everyone was taught the basics as a child, it would take the mystery and fear out of finance. Starting out life with a base understanding would lead to financially healthy behavior, smart decisions, and financial confidence as an adult.

In addition to her CFP, Frazier holds an MBA from Wake Forest University and is a member of the Financial Planning Association and the National Association of Personal Financial Advisors. She joined her family's firm, Frazier Financial Consultants (FFC), in 2014. FFC has been providing money management and financial planning since 1986.

She is also a regular finance contributor on Forbes.com, focusing on everyday personal finance that anyone can understand and use; her articles provide real-world simple, accessible, and entertaining financial advice.

Frazier lives in Westchester, New York, with her husband and children. Outside of work, she can be found playing dinosaurs with her toddler son, on "movie dates" with her five-year-old daughter, conducting science experiments with her nine-year-old stepson, or sneaking away for the much needed date night with husband and friends.

Readers can connect directly with Frazier on her website at lizfrazier .com or on her firm's website at frazierfinancialconsultants.com.